DEM●S

Demos is an independent think tank committed to radical thinking on the long-term problems facing the UK and other advanced industrial societies.

It aims to develop ideas – both theoretical and practical – to help shape the politics of the twenty first century, and to improve the breadth and quality of political debate.

Demos publishes books and a quarterly journal and undertakes substantial empirical and policy oriented research projects. Demos is a registered charity.

In all its work Demos brings together people from a wide range of backgrounds in business, academia, government, the voluntary sector and the media to share and cross-fertilise ideas and experiences.

For further information and
subscription details please contact:
Demos
9 Bridewell Place
London EC4V 6AP
Telephone: 0171 353 4479
Facsimile: 0171 353 4481
email: mail@demos.co.uk

Britain™

Renewing our identity

Mark Leonard

DEMOS

in association with

Design
Council

First published in 1997 by
Demos
9 Bridewell Place
London EC4V 6AP
Telephone: 0171 353 4479
Facsimile: 0171 353 4481
email: mail@demos.co.uk
© Demos 1997

ISBN 1 898309 78 7
Printed in Great Britain by Redwood Books
Cover design by Wolff Olins

Contents

Acknowledgements

I am indebted to the Design Council for funding the research that went into this publication, in particular to John Sorrell, Andrew Summers, Martin Brown, Alison Phillips and Polly Hosp, for advice and assistance. My very special thanks go to Geoff Mulgan who has been an inspiration and guiding light from the beginning to the end of the project, and to Simon Retallack for his sterling research efforts. I must thank Phillip Dodd for providing a wealth of good ideas and generously hosting a series of extremely successful lunches on the topic at the Institute for Contemporary Arts. I am grateful to Tony Smith for his help and generosity in bringing some of the finest minds together to discuss the topic at a seminar in Magdalen College Oxford. I am especially grateful to Wolff Olins for access to their work on the topic and allowing me to use data from their 'made in UK' survey. In particular I would like to thank Wally Olins for sharing his time and vast expertise, Dan Bobby and Robby Laughton for taking me through their 'Branding Britain' project, and Owen Hughes for designing the cover of the report. Very special thanks must also go to Pat Dade, a long-term friend of Demos, for giving us access to unpublished Synergy data, processing it and talking us through its significance. I am also especially grateful to Martin Sandbach and the British Tourist Authority, for giving me access to unpublished BTA data and giving me the benefit of his years of experience at the frontline. I must thank Tom Craig-Cameron and the British Council for access to unpublished British Council data. I must thank Anneke Elwes for setting the debate on 're-branding Britain' in motion a few years ago, and for being so generous with her time and her work. Thanks also to the Henley Centre for allowing me to draw on data from *Frontiers 96* and *Planning for social change*. Special thanks are also due to Linda Colley – a mentor for all students of Britishness – for advice during the project and for the inspired paper she delivered at the Magdalen seminar.

I must also pay tribute to the others who gave their time generously, allowed themselves to be interviewed, contributed to the ICA lunches and the Magdalen seminar, and supplied direction and advice during the course of the project. These include:

Demos

Lord Archer of Weston-super-Mare; Brian Bademan, Diesel; Michael Brown, Fedida Brown Consulting; Professor Peter Carey, Trinity College, Oxford; Professor David Cannadine, Institute for Historical Research; Professor Ian Christie, Magdalen College, Oxford; Michael Clerizo, Cricket; Nigel Coates, Branson Coates Architecture; Bob Cotton, AMX Design; Andrew Davies, Cricket; Mike Dempsey, Director CDT Design; Professor Mary Douglas; Bob Downes, Scottish Enterprise; Greg Dyke, Pearson Television; Adrian Ellis, AEA Consultants; Andrew Fraser, Invest in Britain Bureau; Blair Gibb, Massachusetts Port Authority; Simon Fedida, Fedida Brown Consultancy; Charles Hampden Turner, Judge Institute of Management at Cambridge University; Tom Harris CMG, DTI; Michael Ignatieff; Sunder Katwala, Macmillan; Rodney Kinsman, OMK Design; Janice Kirkpatrick, Graven Images; Professor Harold Koh, All Souls College, Oxford; Graham Leicester, Scottish Council Foundation; Ross Lovegrove; Edmund Marsden, British Council; Tim May, Design House Consultants; David Mercer, British Telecom; John Pawson; Sir David Puttnam CBE; Paul Smith CBE; Professor the Earl Russell; Helen Storey; Charles Trevail, Sampson Tyrrell; John Warwicker, Tomato; Paul Williams, FCO; and Professor Theodore Zeldin, St Anthony's College.

I have drawn from several sources for much of the data in this book, in particular the Central Office of Information's *Britain 1996: an official handbook*, published by HMSO, and *British social attitudes: the 13th report*, published by Social and Community Planning Research and Dartmouth Publishing.

Finally, I must thank all the staff at Demos, in particular Perri 6, Helen Wilkinson, Tom Bentley and Ben Jupp for direction, advice and inspiration, and Lindsay Nash for patience and understanding in the production process and her stylish redesign of our publications.

Mark Leonard
August 1997

Summary

Britain's identity is in flux. Renewed national confidence in the arts, fashion, technology, architecture and design has coincided with the departure from Hong Kong, devolution, further integration with Europe and the imminence of the millennium.

Bad Press

Around the world, however, Britain's image remains stuck in the past.

- Britain is seen as a backward-looking has-been, a theme park world of royal pageantry and rolling green hills, where draft blows through people's houses.
- British products are seen as low tech and bad value: less than 40 per cent of Fortune 500 companies associate British products with being state-of-the-art; under 50 per cent see products 'Made in UK' as offering good value for money.
- British business is seen as strike-ridden and hostile to free trade: over 45 per cent of Fortune 500 companies still associate Britain with poor industrial relations, and under 40 per cent of Japanese companies believe that Britain encourages free enterprise.
- The old stereotypes of Britain having bad weather, poor food and stand-offish people still dominate perceptions

Confused

Within Britain too, our identity is in transition:

- only 50 per cent regard Britishness as an important part of their identity
- The traditional stories of Britishness that were invented in the eighteenth and nineteenth centuries, have lost their resonance. The stories that defined Britishness in terms of institutional continuity and industrial prowess, English language and literature, protestantism, and the invention and domination of sport – today appeal, if at all, only to an ageing minority.
- Faith in our institutions has plummeted: barely 30 per cent think Britain will have a monarchy in 50 years' time; only 10 per cent have confidence in parliament, 25 per cent in the church; and 26 per cent in the legal system.
- Only one in twenty are very proud of our economic achievements.
- Only 27 per cent of British consumers see British products as excellent or good – even the Japanese (32 per cent) have a better regard for British products.
- Britishness embarrasses British business: British Telecom, British Gas, British Home Stores, and the British Airport Authority all dropped the 'British' from their names, and Dixons' own brand MATSUI is meant to sound Japanese.

Backward-looking institutions

Because there is little consensus about what Britain stands for at home, the institutions charged with promoting Britain abroad (Foreign and Commonwealth Office, Department of Trade and Industry, British Tourist Authority, British Council) cannot project a coherent forward-looking image of the country with the £800 million of public money they spend every year. Their activities are fragmented and unstrategic. Often, they opt for the line of least resistance, presenting Britain as a nation of heritage.

The identity premium

Coherent and attractive national identities have political and social benefits. Above all they have an economic value, making it easier for companies to attract investment or win markets. Seventy two per cent of Fortune 500 companies cite national identity as an important influence when purchasing goods and services, and most people will pay over the odds for certain products, such as consumer electronics from Japan, or engineering from Germany. Britain's corporate identity is weak in key areas – particularly innovation and excellence.

'Branding' Britain

Other countries have shown that it is possible to manage identity systematically. Countries as varied as Australia, Spain and Chile have organised concerted campaigns to refashion their identities. Ireland, for example, has rapidly transformed its image from that of a rural, traditional Catholic country to an innovative 'Celtic tiger', with Dublin recast as one of Europe's most exciting cities. There are also important lessons to be learned from businesses which have developed sophisticated techniques for managing their identity.

Shaping our identity

The most important lesson is that the task of renewing identity goes well beyond flags and logos. The key priority is to define a shared ethos, and shared stories, to reflect the best of what Britain has become in the late 1990s. I suggest what some of these stories might be, emphasising Britain's place as a hub, an importer and exporter of ideas, goods and services, people and cultures; Britain's history as a hybrid nation; our traditions of creativity and non-conformism; our role as a silent revolutionary creating new models of organisation; our readiness to do business; and the ethos of fair play and voluntary commitment. These stories should be our trademarks. Together they add up to a new vision of Britain as a global island, uniquely well placed to thrive in the more interconnected world of the next century.

Demos

Projecting our identity

Alongside a new consensus about what Britain stands for and what it means to be British, we will also need new mechanisms to manage our identity. This report argues for:

- *coordination:* establish a small vision group chaired by the Prime Minister to agree strategic objectives and a working party with representatives from all the agencies – government and business – involved in promoting Britain abroad, to ensure that consistent messages are used.
- *professionalisation:* establish a 'Promoting Britain Unit' based in the Cabinet Office to provide logistical support, systematically measure performance and track our identity.
- *cultural changes:* implement new approaches to recruitment and organisation to make Britain's institutions more entrepreneurial, more long term, more creative and more representative of Britain's contemporary diversity.

The millennium as a focus

The millennium provides a unique opportunity to project a new image of Britain to the world, reflecting these new stories in events, buildings and exhibitions. We should capitalise on it by:

- redesigning airports and stations, and entrance points such as the Channel Tunnel, to provide visitors with a stunning welcome to the country and immediate contact with the best contemporary art and design
- developing the world's most impressive web sites to provide an introduction to Britain, linked in with web sites for the major cities and including not only public information but also discussion groups, arts, listings and tourism information.
- beginning a programme to transform Britain's buildings around the world – from embassies to British Council offices – to further the transition from a backward-looking imperial style. We should

also review stamps, letterheads and official documents to achieve a better mix between old and new.

■ building a model 'living museum of the future' – a real global village or 'Millennium City' in Greenwich to act as a showcase of the future of health, learning, retailing and democracy, and to situate the UK as a laboratory of future ways of living.

■ organising a tour by the monarch of all sites where there is still bitterness about Britain's past – from Ireland to Iran – to heal difficult memories and to signal that Britain has moved beyond its imperial heritage.

■ establishing a 'Commitments' web site, accessible in the Millennium Dome and in all places associated with the millennium, to provide new opportunities to commit to volunteering and mentoring, both within the UK and across national boundaries

Re-imagining Britain

The renewal of identity does not imply casting off what has gone before. Our challenge is to find a better fit between our heritage and what we are becoming. The time is now ripe for Britain to do that. Britain has a spring in its step and a new mood of confidence. Two hundred years ago our ancestors invented a new identity that proved enormously successful. They pioneered new institutions, new images and new ways of thinking, free from any sentimental attachment to the traditions they had inherited. Today we need to do the same again.

Introduction:
redesigning UK plc

Britain has a new spring in its step. National success in creative industries like music, design and architecture has combined with steady economic growth to dispel much of the introversion and pessimism of recent decades. 'Cool Britannia' sets the pace in everything from food to fashion.

Yet around the world Britain continues to be seen in a very different light: backward-looking and hidebound, arrogant and aloof. The world's business community ranks Britain's industries as less innovative and committed to quality than our competitors, while the world's tourists view Britain as a worthy – but dull – destination.

Within Britain, too, there is considerable confusion about what Britain will be, or will stand for, in the future. The arguments about Europe, the sentiments felt over the handover of Hong Kong to China, the uncertainties about how to celebrate the millennium – all are symptoms of a national identity in transition.

This report does not claim to address all of the subtle and complex dimensions of our national identity. But it does argue that there is an important gap between Britain's great strengths – as an innovator, a producer, a seller of services, a tolerant and creative society – and the identity we project to the outside world. Moreover, it argues that we now have a unique opportunity to bridge that gap, refashioning our identity to bring it closer into line with what Britain has become in the late 1990s.

What should that identity be? What should we take with us into a new century and what should we leave behind?

In this book I do not offer a full answer to that question – although I do map out many of the elements that might contribute to it. Instead, I examine what role a national identity has for the people who live and work in a nation and for those who visit it or trade with it. I look at the institutions that manage the identity. I examine how malleable or fixed identities are. I draw lessons from how other countries have refashioned themselves and examine how techniques developed by companies to manage identities can be used to 'brand' countries. Finally, I suggest some of the qualities that might contribute to a renewed identity – qualities that make sense of our future as well as our past.

Part 1. The facts

Nations have been recreating their identities throughout recorded history. Monarchs, emperors, popes and parliaments all used icons, myths and ceremonies to tell the world what they stood for and what made them special. Today, nations use new tools – logos and branding techniques, advertising campaigns and festivals, speeches and trade fairs – to project their identity to the outside world.

This report will argue that the time is ripe to use some of these tools. Other nations – from Spain to Ireland, Australia to Singapore – have successfully renewed their identities in recent years and there are important lessons to be learned from the business world which now manages corporate identities far more systematically and professionally than in the past.

But the main reason why this needs to be done is that a gulf has opened up between the reality of Britain as a highly creative and diverse society and the perception around the world that Britain remains a backward-looking island immersed in its heritage.

What is our foreign image?

In the past, Britain had an extraordinarily strong external image. It might often have been resented, but Britain's prowess as an industrial and military power was always respected. Today, that identity has become confused and outdated and, in many parts of the world, decades of relative decline have left the word 'Britain' meaning very little. To anyone living in Britain, it comes as something of a shock to discover just how little 'brand recognition' we have.[1] Despite a volley of features in *Time* magazine, the *New York Times*, *Newsweek*, *Vanity Fair* and many European and Asian journals heralding the rebirth of

London as the world's coolest capital, Britain's 'renaissance' has passed by much of the rest of the world. To most people in China or Brazil, and even to many in the United States or Russia, Britain has neither a positive nor a negative image. It simply has no clear image at all.

Moreover, where Britain is recognised, it is seen as a country whose time has come and gone – bogged down by tradition, riven by class and threatened by industrial disputes, the IRA and poverty-stricken inner cities.[2] The British people, meanwhile, are seen as insular, cold and arrogant – the inhabitants of a theme park world of royal pageantry, rolling green hills and the changing of the guard.[3]

'We are still seen as the snobbiest nation in the world. Foreigners hate that – they think "who the hell are you!"'[1]
Lord Archer of Weston-super-mare

There is a remarkable consistency in the clichés that characterise our image abroad, although the further a country is from Britain, the more one-dimensional its view of Britishness will be.

The Europeans, who are near and make up over 60 per cent of our trade and 70 per cent of tourists, have the most sophisticated picture of us.[4] They see the subtleties in our geographical and social profile. There is a clear consensus about what we are good at: music, comedy, literature, drama, media, advertising, social trends, fashion, advertising, finance and caring for homes and gardens.[5] Equally clear is the consensus about what we are bad at: food, dressing, social politics and being European.[6]

In Asia, there is a less tolerant view. Many Asians regard Britain as trapped in the past and closed to the world. Fewer than 40 per cent of Japanese believe that Britain encourages free enterprise – and even in pro-British Hong Kong the figure is barely 65 per cent.[7] At the same time, over 80 per cent of the citizens in Hong Kong, Indonesia, Japan, Korea, Malaysia, the Philippines and Thailand see Britain's reputation for innovation and creativity as based more on the past than the present.[8] They recognise our strengths as well – but mainly those rooted in the past. Britain is seen as a country which respects the rights of its ethnic minorities, has an excellent standard of higher education and is a model of democracy (except in the opinion of China). The flip side of the coin is that a majority in China, Hong Kong, Indonesia, Malaysia and the Philippines think that the British media lie.[9]

The Americans have a remarkably limited view of what Britain stands for. For most, the special relationship isn't very special. Research shows a medley of imagery and associations – croquet, tea-time, Robin Hood, tweed, castles, Henry VIII, thatched cottages, stormy seas, Charles Dickens' London, pretty gardens, jaded aristocracy, James Bond, Beefeaters, Shakespeare and Eton.[10] Americans see us through the lens of Merchant Ivory productions as a class-ridden society, the preserve of unchanging traditional values and a pretty and contained countryside – the antithesis of the wild US with its unmanageable and mythical outdoors. There is a sense that Britain and its institutions are a performance held to entertain the world and a recent *New York Times* editorial claimed that 'the British royal family exist for *our* amusement'. The only recent addition to this set of images is that English accents have become standard-issue for Hollywood villains.

On the other side of the world, Australia and New Zealand see Britain as their polar opposite in terms of attitudes as well as geography: bad at progressiveness, equality, emotional warmth, enjoying life and being open to the outside world. Antipodeans hold the same quaint and conservative picture of British country life as Americans, but this is intruded on by more urban images of darkness, dirt and overcrowding.[11] Though British art and media are familiar and admired, perceptions tend to be dominated by beer, cars, street fashion, finance and literature.[12]

The overall story is that most see Britain as a backward-looking place, an old country living off its capital.

Some might argue that this doesn't matter. After all, many people around the world respect Britain for its continuity and stability. To assess the effects of this image I look at its economic significance in three fields: Britain's place as an exporter, as a tourist destination, and as a site for inward investment.

Export Britain: old fashioned, poor quality?
Britain is home to a disproportionate number of world class companies, from Glaxo-Wellcome to ICI, Shell and BP to Grand

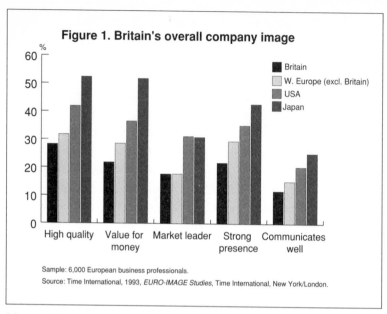

Figure 1. Britain's overall company image

Sample: 6,000 European business professionals.
Source: Time International, 1993, *EURO-IMAGE Studies*, Time International, New York/London.

Metropolitan. Yet the overall image of our companies lags far behind the rest of Europe, the United States and Japan – scraping barely half the Japanese score on every attribute (see Figure 1).

Even in markets where we perform well, we are some way behind – seventh for car manufacturing, fifth for beer and third for fashion (but far behind France and Italy).[13] Recognition of our companies' brands is also weak – only three British companies and one Anglo-Dutch Company (Shell, no 3; BP, No15; Jaguar, no 42; Rolls Royce, no 47) are among the top 50 in a ranking of most familiar companies worldwide by 6,000 European business professionals.[14] All of these brands pre-date the Second World War.

Throughout the world, the British are seen to excel in areas that are rooted in the past. In Europe, these include packaged and traditional foods (jams, pies, pastry, sweets, biscuits, puddings, preserves, smoked salmon, tea and chocolate) and classic craftsmanship (clothes, shoes, sports cars and motorbikes).[15] In Australia and New Zealand, the brands that are recognised originate from 1950s England.[16]

Research shows that Britain has also been hampered by the structural fragmentation of its economy. Examples of British excellence are not clustered around particular sectors of the economy or cul-

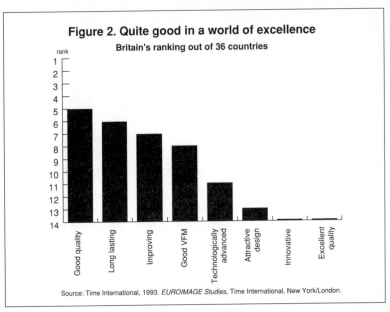

Figure 2. Quite good in a world of excellence

Britain's ranking out of 36 countries

Source: Time International, 1993. *EUROIMAGE Studies*, Time International, New York/London.

tural life. There are few companies or sectors of the economy which dominate the world market in the way that Japanese (in robotics), German (in printing presses) or American (in film and specialised medical equipment) industries do. Britain tends to excel in niches at the higher end of a wide range of sectors (for example, Linn products and NAD in hi-fi equipment, Rolls Royce and Cosworth at the high end of the automotive industry).[17]

Overall, British products are seen as among the safest, but also among the least enjoyable, and British companies have failed to build a reputation for excellence.[18] Research shows that while it is possible to build up a reputation for good quality on the past and tradition, excellence is associated with the future. This matters, because in a competitive global economy, being quite good is often not enough.

Tourist Britain: bad food, poor weather and stand-offish people?
Research by the British Tourist Authority (BTA) shows that there is no single or clear perception of Britain in many countries. A major qualitative survey of attitudes in six countries (the Netherlands, the United States, Singapore, Australia, Italy and Germany) revealed a startling lack of knowledge, particularly among Americans and

younger people in all countries except Singapore. The Dutch are the most familiar with Britain but even they could not recognise the shape of Britain on a map. The problem, surprisingly, is not just that there are negative perceptions, but rather that there are no perceptions for a generation that cannot remember Britain's role in the Second World War or as a great power.

Among those familiar with the UK, there were powerful reasons for not visiting: the weather, the people, the food, the dangers, the dullness and the political record. But although British people are perceived as unfriendly and arrogant, those who visit the country tend to leave with a better impression than when they arrived. Again, our dogged reputation for bad quality and sloppy food is tempered among those who have experienced modern British cuisine. The general perception that the UK, and London in particular, is not a safe place, with people living under the shadow of IRA bombs, homeless on the streets and racial tensions is also (at least partially) relieved among those who have experienced the country.

Perhaps more worrying is the perception that Britain is dull. In fact, many people in the BTA survey, in particular younger ones, were bemused by the idea of Britain as a holiday destination, seeing it as the preserve of history, heritage, the monarchy and reserve with nothing to attract new visitors. Here again most people who had visited Britain found it more interesting than anticipated. Britain also suffers from a negative political image. This applies both to Europe, where we have been seen as an 'awkward partner' and a 'bad European', and also across the world in areas where we are still resented for our imperial past.

Research shows that the idea of a 'creative' Britain was simply not credible to many of the people surveyed. When surveyed recently, only a small minority of younger people in the US, Holland and Australia had heard of the modern British revival. If creative meant anything in relation to Britain, it was associated with high culture.

Despite these image problems, however, Britain is doing well as a tourist destination: it is ranked fifth in the world tourism market and the international Passenger Survey shows that 26 million people visited the UK in 1996 (up 8 per cent on 1995), spending £12.7 billion (up 5 per cent on 1995).

Why, then, do people come? 'Tradition' is seen as the most credible single label for Britain and has crowded out any other images. There is a general perception that we have clung on to things that the rest of the world disposed of years ago. We have houses through which drafts blow, ubiquitous dirt and arcane rituals. Though many visitors are attracted by the scenery – cliffs, green fields, English country gardens, Scottish moorlands, exciting, powerful romantic images that come from novels and films – they see this within the context of history and tradition. Many visitors, particularly from younger countries or countries which have had to bury their pasts, enjoy the indulgence of a country which glories in its history and traditions. People from the new world and former colonies are also attracted to the mores and institutions that formed the staple of their educational and cultural life – from the landmarks of literature to the squares on the Monopoly board. The great majority want Britain to deliver accessible history through sightseeing and the sacred icons of well-known buildings and monuments. Meanwhile some people, particularly from Asia, come to Britain for a view of life in a 'democratic society'.

'I always felt that the reason why people bought Minis was because they were very much tied up with "Swinging London" … it helped sell British fashions, in the same way that Punk and the Sex Pistols helped sell Vivienne Westwood.'

Peter Jenner,
Sincere Management

Who visits? The majority of tourists are Dinkies (Double income, no kids) and Dippies (Double income pensioners). Tourists from Asia have a younger profile and consist mainly of 'office ladies'. From Europe, visitors range from young 'women behaving badly' from Norway, who abandon husbands and children for serious shopping and fun (the tour operators' slogan is blatant: 'Dump husbands and have a good weekend!') to the growing numbers of Italian and French teenagers who are attracted by street fashion, London clothes markets (Portobello, Camden), trendy bars, dressy clubs, way out catwalk designers and artists (Alexander McQueen, Vivienne Westwood) and a rich music scene (Britpop, rave). But this picture of Britain is not well known and opportunities in emerging markets – such as Generation X in California – are being squandered as people

Demos

whose holiday expectations and desires match London perfectly are choosing to go elsewhere.

Invest in Britain: low-tech, bad value, strike-ridden?
Although Britain has been successful in attracting inward investment, our image in the business world is often either negative or virtually non-existent. A survey of 200 of the world's leading companies (Fortune 500 companies) revealed that only 36 per cent felt the label 'Made in UK' would positively influence their purchasing decisions for goods and services, 7 per cent said that it would be a negative influence and 57 per cent, despite being influenced by the national image, were immune or indifferent to the UK.[19] More worrying was the detail of companies' perceptions. Over 45 per cent of companies still associate the UK with poor industrial relations (compared to only 39 per cent who do not) and only 53 per cent of companies recognise that the UK has succeeded in securing a low inflation economy.[20] Less than half of manufacturing companies think that products made in UK offer good value for money and less than 40 per cent associate British products with being state-of-the-art. This is reflected in the sectors that are associated with the UK – unprompted, 40 per cent of manufacturers associated the UK with the automotive sector, followed by clothing and textiles.[21] When prompted, the strongest associations were with financial services, closely followed by drinks, media, automotive manufacturing and tourism and heritage (96 per cent of US companies and 87 per cent of Far East companies associate these with the UK).[22] Less than one third of those surveyed associated the UK with consumer electronics and, surprisingly, 64 per cent saw no connection with architecture.[23]

Some of the results are more positive. Fifty seven per cent of companies felt that the image of UK industry has improved over the last few years. Two thirds of manufacturing companies regard UK-produced goods as well designed, and in the Far-East this rises to 73 per cent.[24] Sixty per cent of companies see the UK as having world class management and the same percentage associate it with a highly skilled workforce.[25] Over 75 per cent of manufacturers think that the UK has an international perspective and the UK is the most popular nation in Europe among manufacturers for commercial and trading partnerships.[26] In a survey of 36 countries, Britain was the fifth most popular country to do business with.[27]

So the overall picture is mixed. There are strong and important positive perceptions. But there are also 'negatives' that need to be countered if Britain's full economic potential is to be realised.

What has happened to Britishness?

In practice, external images are not easily separable from internal perceptions. Often external images simply reflect how countries see themselves – usually lagging by a generation. If we are to understand our image abroad, we must see how it is mirrored in what the British themselves think of their identity.

Whereas in the past Britishness was a compelling part of people's make-up – not surprisingly, since successive generations had to risk their lives to fight for the nation – today such national identities are being eclipsed by more personal identities (see Figure 3). When ranking the most important components of identity, people cite 'my principles and values' (66 per cent), 'my interests' (61 per cent),

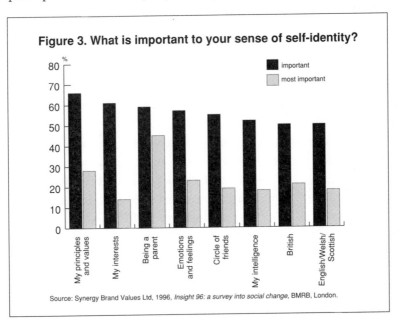

Figure 3. What is important to your sense of self-identity?

Source: Synergy Brand Values Ltd, 1996, *Insight 96: a survey into social change*, BMRB, London.

Figure 4. Britishness still matters				
'How close do you feel to...'		(percentages)		
	Very close	**Close**	**Not very close**	**Not close at all**
your neighbourhood (or village)	**16.5**	**43.7**	**24.9**	**9.3**
your town or city	10.3	40.0	31.8	9.5
your county	**9.4**	**35.0**	**32.8**	**12.8**
Britain	21.1	41.9	19.2	8.1
Europe	**3.2**	**15.9**	**36.1**	**31.7**

Source: Jowell et al, eds, 1996, *British social attitudes*, Social and Community Planning Research and Dartmouth Publishing, Aldershot.

'being a parent' (59 per cent), 'emotions and feelings' (57 per cent), 'circle of friends' (55 per cent) and 'my intelligence' (52 per cent) as more important than Britishness.[28] Barely half of the population see Britishness as an important feature of their identity,[29] and roughly as many rate being English, Scottish or Welsh as important.[30]

But it would be wrong to conclude that Britishness is ceasing to count or that the UK is decomposing back to its component parts. It is true that in an era of peace national identities matter less. But a sense of belonging is still important to people. The *British social attitudes* survey found that when respondents were asked how close they felt to particular localities (neighbourhoods, towns and cities) all scored relatively highly but Britishness came out as much the strongest single attachment.

The origins of Britishness

To understand what Britishness means today – and what it could mean in the future – we need to understand how we got here and how Britain developed that traditional identity which still remains so strong around the world. Far from having had 1,000 years of unbroken continuity, Britain – and Britishness – are relatively recent and deliberately constructed creations. Historians have taught us that Britishness, which had been germinating at least since the formal incorporation of Wales in 1536,

'Looking back is always more appealing than looking forward ... the future is threatening'
Martin Sandbach,
British Tourist Authority

only took firm root through a dynastic accident in 1603 when James VI of Scotland became James I of England. In fact, though there was a British monarch from then onwards, before the Act of Union in 1707 there was no British state (the Scots couldn't tax the English and the English couldn't tax the Scots). There were separate currencies (with a fixed exchange rate), separate legal and education systems, separate religions and even separate coronations (though the monarchs would often take a number of years to get round to the Scottish part of their coronation). The Act of Union establishing Britain as a political entity reads more like an international agreement than a constitution, with clauses stating that Westminster may not tamper with the Church of Scotland or the membership of the Court of Session or make Scottish cases triable by English law or destroy the separate seal of Scotland, along with a requirement to maintain separate mints and notes.[31]

As Linda Colley points out in her book *Britons: the forging of a nation*, the British national interest forged in the eighteenth century was not inherited but learned. As a nation, Britain was held together by the combination of patronage and cash, on the one

---

Figure 5. The invention of Britain

● Incorporation of Wales in 1536

● Union of the Crowns in 1603

● Act of Union in 1707

● British national anthem composed in 1740

● Union Jack designed and first used in its modern form in 1801

● First celebration of a royal jubilee in 1809

● Inauguration of the National Portrait Gallery in 1856

● Reinvention of Queen Victoria as Empress of India in 1877

● Founding of the National Trust in 1895

● First BA in English Literature at Oxford University awarded in 1896

● Founding of the BBC in the mid-1920s

● Royal Christmas broadcast first instituted in 1932

---

hand, and common threats on the other. The threats came from Catholicism and France. The opportunities came from trade and empire, and it was often Welshmen and Scotsmen who benefited most from the jobs and the trading opportunities of empire, just as it was they who became the most ardent advocates of British identity. Indeed it was a Welshman who coined the term 'British Empire' and the Scot or Welsh-led Labour and Liberal Parties which were the parties of 'Britain'.[32]

'The English will either speak of Britain and mean England – or they will deny the existence of the Union.'
Lord Conrad Russell

It is common to assume that national identities emerge naturally. In fact, British identity did not grow unaided. A succession of national institutions and traditions were consciously invented or reformed to give it shape: Parliament, the monarchy, the British Army, the National Portrait Gallery, the reinvention of Queen Victoria as Empress of India, the National Trust and so on.

As the institutions of Britishness developed, Britain's constituent parts had to reinvent themselves and make sense of what Englishness, Welshness and Scottishness meant under new circumstances. Highland dress, for example was invented by an Englishman after the Union of 1707, the differentiated 'class tartans' are an even later invention and the word 'kilt' didn't exist until twenty years after the Union.[33]

Together, the new institutions and icons of Britishness melded into an extremely robust identity. They crystallised just as Britain rose to success as an imperial and industrial power and they gave British citizens an extraordinary confidence and pride. Today, however, each of the pillars on which that identity rests has been eroded.

Institutions

The first pillar is our institutional heritage. Visitors to London often send home postcards of the Houses of Parliament ('the mother of all parliaments') or Buckingham Palace. They intuitively understand that Britain is a nation held together by its central institutions. Few visitors to France or Germany send postcards of central government institutions. The Conservative MP David Willetts has made this case very strongly: 'France gets through republics the way Hollywood stars get through marriages. The intense national pride felt by a Frenchman ... has more to do with culture and cuisine, than with the vagaries of political institutions ... The British case is different. We have a much longer history ... of established institutions than any of the continental countries ... the sovereignty of the monarch in Parliament is a fundamental part of the British historical tradition. The Palace of Westminster is a much more vivid symbol of British nationhood than the German or French assemblies.'[34]

There is undoubtedly an important truth in this argument. But to the extent that it is accurate it only highlights the fact that when Britain's institutions run into problems the national identity does too. Today, even the most ardent advocate of tradition cannot be blind to the problems of legitimacy that so many of Britain's oldest institutions are suffering (see Figure 6). The royal family sometimes looks more like a comic soap opera rather than a source of envy – only 13 per cent of British people 'respect' it[35] and 45 per cent do not think that Britain will have a monarchy in 50 years' time, compared to only 30 per cent who think it will.[36] The judiciary, Parliament and

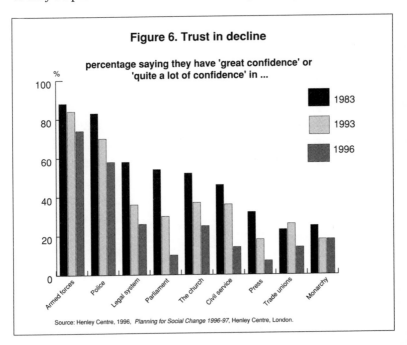

Figure 6. Trust in decline

percentage saying they have 'great confidence' or 'quite a lot of confidence' in ...

Source: Henley Centre, 1996, *Planning for Social Change 1996-97*, Henley Centre, London.

the Treasury have been undermined by a series of high-profile fail-
ures. Between 1983 and 1996, the percentage of people who had
'great confidence' or 'quite a lot of confidence' in Parliament
dropped from 54 per cent to 10 per cent; confidence in the legal system fell from 58 per cent to 26 per cent; in the church from 52 per
cent to 25 per cent and in the civil service from 46 per cent to 14 per
cent.[37] The proportion of people who trusted government ministers
to tell the truth fell to 10 per cent.[38] Deference towards ancient customs has also steadily eroded – 74 per cent disagree with the statement that 'fox hunting is traditional to the English way of life and
should be encouraged'.[39] Even the Union Jack has become an ambiva-
lent symbol – at times a racist icon for skinheads and fascists.

Other institutions that played a key role in cementing a national
consciousness, such as the BBC and nationalised industries, have
also been either weakened or detached from their national role. The
rise of satellite and cable television means that the BBC can never
again portray itself as the voice of the nation, defining its culture
and even its accent in singular terms. Commercial pressures on the
BBC to develop global business ventures have also made it less of a
national, public institution. At the same time privatisation has
diluted the 'Britishness' of a series of utilities. John Betjeman once
remarked that Britain was founded on 'democracy and drains', and
the great civic and municipal institutions that took shape in the last
century were without doubt an important part of Britain's sense of
itself as a progressive and fair society. More than a decade of privatisation has left a very different landscape. British Gas has
spawned Centrica, British Telecom has become BT and now Concert,
British Airways is energetically recasting itself as a carrier of a global, rather than a national, culture and our drains are as likely to be
run by a French company working under contract as by a British
utility.

Empire

The second pillar was the empire. In 1997 the fiftieth anniversary of
the loss of the Raj coincides with Britain's final departure from
Hong Kong. Barely 50 years ago, 800 million people lived in the
British Empire. Today (if we leave aside the population of the UK),

the figure is 168,000.[40] The trauma of coming to terms with our role as a middle-ranking power in the world has dominated much of our post-war politics but the empire is not even a distant memory for most people living in Britain today. The fact that the army has failed to recruit 15,000 of the 46,000 young people it needs to carry out its tasks (and expects even worse recruitment problems in the future) shows that young people have outgrown imperial ambition.[41] Yet everywhere we look, we are surrounded by its legacy – from the honours system ('Order of the British Empire' and 'Medal of the British Empire') to ICI (Imperial Chemical Industries), the Foreign and Commonwealth Office (FCO) to distant, long-forgotten dependencies like Montserrat. As Yasmin Alibhai-Brown recently wrote in relation to Hong Kong, 'The protracted, extravagant requiem for the last colony proved that imperial fantasies still haunt and deeply affect the self-image of this country.'[42]

Industry

The third pillar of our identity has been industry. One hundred or even fifty years ago, Britishness meant industry. At the Great Exhibition of 1851, the organisers were happy to put on display the world's finest products because they could be confident that the British ones would stand out. Today, despite some of the rhetoric of the 1980s, only one in twenty (5.5 per cent)[43] of the public are very proud of our economic achievements and British consumers are notoriously unpatriotic: 27 per cent of UK consumers think that British products are excellent or good, compared to 38 per cent who think this of German products and 43 per cent of Japanese products.[44] Contrast this with Japan, where 75 per cent think home produced products are excellent or very good, France, where the figure is 45 per cent, or even China, where 39 per cent support their own products.[45] In fact, British products are more valued in Hungary (62 per cent), India (38 per cent), Thailand (32 per cent) and Japan

> 'Companies get too caught up with old Britain. We don't appreciate the value of Britain. In Holland, the Dutch telecom company fears BT as it is a hugely successful company – here we say 'stupid piper'. We have some great organisations: BHS, BG, BAA, BTG – most have dropped "British" from their names'
>
> Charles Trevail, Sampson Tyrrell

(32 per cent) than they are here.[46] To British business, the archaic identity of a declining middle power has become an embarrassing burden. Such is the stigma attached to Britishness in many markets that the retailer Dixons, when deciding on a name for its own brand products, plumped for MATSUI, concluding that to sell consumer electronics successfully it would have to pretend to be Japanese.

Language

The fourth pillar is language. The English language was a powerful unifying force in the seventeenth and eighteenth centuries. Today, although 84 per cent agree that it is very or fairly important to be able to speak English to be truly British, English has become an international language.[47] It is the most rapidly evolving language in the world and the vast majority of new vocabulary comes from outside the UK – there is no longer a sense that we have ownership of it. Indeed it has become a cliché that the Dutch and the Swedes speak English better than native speakers, while the Indians and Australians write it better than the British.

Culture and religion

The fifth pillar is religion and culture. Two hundred years ago, the new Britain was very consciously a Protestant nation. Today, barely 30 per cent see being a Christian as important or fairly important for being truly British[48] – and only 68 per cent consider themselves Christian.[49] The role of the media has also had a massive effect on identity. The great unifiers built up at the beginning of the century to ensure a common and shared culture for the British people have been rapidly undermined. The growth of satellite and digital television will be the death knell of a society that watches the same programmes and absorbs the same information every day. Yet people remain proud of our culture – 68 per cent are very or somewhat proud of Britain's achievements in the arts and literature.[50] And people still see it as important component of identity – 70 per cent think that 'it is impossible for people who do not share British customs and traditions to become truly British'.[51]

Sport

The sixth pillar is sport. This has been central to many diverse pictures of Britishness past. The thwack of leather on willow has passed into cliché and sport has acted as a fount of assumed superiority to other countries, with games from football to cricket – given rules by the public schools of England – being copied throughout the world. Indeed the role of the British as missionaries for sport is still evident in the anglicised names of the world's biggest football clubs, such as AC Milan.[52] Sport has also been used as a means of discovering who the 'real Brits' are, most famously in Norman Tebbit's 'cricket test', which claimed that members of Britain's ethnic minorities who cheered the Pakistani, Indian or West Indian cricket teams were not truly British. At a deeper level sport has been seen as essential to the political peace in Britain, with the much vaunted spirit of fair play infusing our language and institutions.

The role of sport has, however, radically changed through the years. When ball-tampering allegations are no longer aimed only at Pakistanis but at the captain of the England team itself and when British footballers are accused of match rigging and violence, British fair play is under threat. When other countries started regularly beating us at the sports that we invented, superiority was challenged and was often greeted with violence. And, barely ten years after Tebbit's test, sport has become a national unifier rather than a source of conflict. In many of the major cities, working-class racism has been challenged directly and overcome by hero-worship of John Barnes, Eric Cantona, Juninho and others, and the record of tackling racism and promoting multiculturalism in other sports is also impressive. Despite these changes to the role of sport, Eric Hobsbawm's dictum that 'the imagined community of millions seems more real as a team of eleven named individuals',[53] still holds true in a country where 70 per cent are very or somewhat proud of Britain's achievements in sports, and 90 per cent claim to feel proud to be British 'when British athletes do well in international sports'.[54] So sport retains its ability to symbolise and strengthen national identity, though it can no longer be a source of difference from the rest of the world.

The generation gap

The cumulative result of all of these pressures on the old ideas of Britishness is a generational split over what Britishness means. Traditional stories of Britain exclude not only ethnic minorities but also large sections of the population who do not remember the war and who have grown up with different values. Surveys indicate that those who see Britishness as an important part of their identity tend to be over 55, male and have few educational qualifications.[55] Many of their conceptions of Britain were forged in the pre-war, war and immediate post-war era, and are rooted in tradition, hierarchy, deference and nostalgia for an era of fixed certainties. They subscribe to a fairly traditional story of British identity – values which look to the past and are now on the wane.

'Only 37 per cent of eighteen to 34 year olds believe that "Britain is a better country than most other countries"'

British social attitudes: the 13th report

This group has an exclusive patriotism that sees Britain as the best in the world and views other ethnicities as a threat. The *British social attitudes* survey found that 61 per cent of people over 60 strongly agree that they 'would rather be a citizen of Britain than of any other country in the world' compared to 28 per cent of eighteen to 34 year olds. Seventy per cent of over 55s agree that 'Britain is a better country than most other countries', compared to 37 per cent of eighteen to 34 year olds.

This is allied to hostility towards foreigners, with 71 per cent of over 55s agreeing that Britain should limit the import of foreign products to protect its national economy (compared to 46 per cent of eighteen to 24 year olds), and almost twice as many over 65s (50 per cent) as eighteen to 44 year olds (27 per cent) feel that foreigners should not be allowed to buy land in Britain. Generational attitudes towards foreigners living in Britain differ just as much. One in three over 65s agree that it is impossible for people who do not share British customs and traditions to become fully British compared to one in twenty eighteen to 24 year olds. Three quarters of 55 to 59 years olds (and only a few percentage points fewer of over 60s) believe that it is better for society if different racial and ethnic groups adapt and blend into the larger society rather than maintain their distinct customs and traditions, compared to under half of eighteen to 24 year olds.

The older generations are also more attached to the institutions that define traditional Britishness. Eighty five per cent of over 55s are proud of British history, 86 per cent of Britain's armed forces and 68 per cent of the way our democracy works, compared to only 7.5 per cent of eighteen to 44 year olds. Over half (51 per cent) of over 55s are proud of Britain's political influence in the world, compared to just over one third (36 per cent) of eighteen to 24 year olds. And the key tenet of Britain's post-war order – our social security system – is a source of pride for 53 per cent of over 55s compared to 34 per cent of eighteen to 34 year olds.

There is also a generational split over the importance of Christianity as a component of British identity: only 11.5 per cent of eighteen to 34 year olds believe that it is important to be Christian to be truly British (4 per cent see it as very important), compared to 63 per cent of over 65 year olds who see it as important and 46 per cent who see it as very important.

> 'If young English people grow up to believe that they do not have a culture in which they can legitimately take pride, their natural group instinct may find an outlet in jingoism, racism and violence'
>
> Clive Aslet, author of *Anyone for England*

Finally, older people are also more attached to Britain as a geographical entity. Sixty per cent of over 55s believe that it is important to have been born in Britain in order to be truly British, compared to 37 per cent of eighteen to 34 year olds, and 60 to 64 year olds are also by far the most unwilling to move outside Britain – only 8.5 per cent would consider it if it were financially advantageous – compared to 31.5 per cent of 25 to 34 year olds. Given their age, this section of the population and the values they hold are destined to represent an ever-smaller proportion of the population and the British identity they espouse will become less relevant. However, there is still no story of Britishness that reflects the softer and more open values of the generation that will replace them.

Demos

How do our institutions project our identity?

Given the confusion over our identity both at home and abroad, it is not surprising that the agencies charged with managing it have a difficult job. Yet these agencies operate with substantial budgets and significant influence. In total, almost £800 million of public money is spent on Britain's identity. This includes the Foreign Office (£15 million on information), the Department of Trade and Industry (DTI – £55 million on export promotion), the British Council (£420 million), the Invest in Britain Bureau, the British Tourist Authority (£35 million) and the BBC (£52 million on the World Service and £189 million on World Service Television). One can add to that a slice at least of the £10 billion spent each year by British companies on advertising their products at home and abroad.[56]

'Our identity is simply not managed ... there is an initiative a week – nothing resembling an industrial policy or strategic planning'

Adrian Ellis, AEA consultants

These substantial sums clearly achieve some successes in attracting investors and consumers, tourists and opinion formers. But, because there is no consensus in Britain about what British identity will be about in the future, our institutions have been unable to project a single, coherent, forward-looking image of Britain abroad. Instead, they have often opted for the line of least resistance and built up what in the commercial world would be called a 'strong brand equity' based around tradition. Government has led the way with archaic and ageing diplomatic missions filled with Chippendale furniture; pompous heraldry on official publications; titled diplomatic envoys; tourism advertising displays of thatched pubs and classic cars; and cardboard cut-out Beefeaters at trade fairs. The image has been reinforced by films in the Merchant Ivory mould – marketed by the BBC's US subsidiary Lionheart Television – and by advertising campaigns for premium products from Jaguar and Scotch whisky. Entry and exit points to the country have conveyed the same message, from footage of green rolling hills and royal pageantry played to British Airways passengers to the goods of traditional Britain – smoked salmon, luxury jam, tea caddies, malt whiskies – on sale at airports and stations. Even many of the attempts to celebrate Britishness within the country have been backward-looking and clumsy, the misfiring of the D-Day celebrations being a classic example.

Research funded by the DTI, the Design Council and the British Council has shown that, because there is no common story of the future, there is very little coordination between the different bodies charged with selling Britain abroad. In the words of a recent report by AEA. 'significant opportunities [are] missed as each player continues to invest in its own necessarily short-term and fragmented programme activities. Opportunities are lost both for economies of scale and for the chance to build a coherent, themed, mutually reinforcing programme of events'.[57] Another problem that AEA highlighted is a lack of consistency in agencies' outputs. By trying to cut costs through competitive tendering and by trying to shift costs out on to industry, the government has left every show with different design components and a different focus. As one businessman put it: 'The British stall at Seville trade fair looked like an M&S clearance sale!'

Over the past few years things have been getting better. Emblematic companies such as Jaguar and British Airways have realised that they can't rely on tradition alone and have begun to foster more consciously modern and dynamic images. Jaguar has emphasised the quality of its technology and British Airways is self-consciously projecting a forward-looking, multicultural open identity.

There has also been a flurry of activity from public agencies. The FCO has set up a specific public diplomacy division and is cooperating with sections of the DTI to take a more integrated view of Britain's image abroad. Their information department commissions TV, radio and print newsfeeds (such as British Satellite News – a 10-minute newsfeed produced daily and used by 75 stations and syndicators, radio programmes like the Russian language 'Big Ben iz Londona' and the overseas press which provides news stories on any theme, in any language, with pictures); publishes 160 titles in nineteen languages; organises exhibitions; hosts 2,500 overseas visitors a year; briefs and trains mission staff; briefs the 2,000 London correspondents of foreign papers and even publishes on the Internet. The

DTI spends £55 million on export promotion every year and employs, with the FCO, 2,000 staff overseas simply to promote exports. The BTA has 43 offices in 37 countries around the world dedicated to encouraging people to take holidays in Britain. At the same time, the British Council operates in 228 towns in 109 countries, employs 1,400 teachers, supports more than 2,000 arts and literature festivals, runs 185 libraries and information centres, and organises (with the DTI and DfEE) export missions, fairs and exhibitions and seminars in over 50 countries.[58]

> 'There are a lot of boring pin-striped people in our institutions. You'll have to kick 'em to death before they work properly'
>
> Lord Archer of Weston-super-mare

Most of the time the different agencies work in parallel or wholly separately. Sometimes they cooperate and when this is done well the results can be impressive. In Korea, for example, a one-stop shop was recently set up merging the services offered by the British Council, the BTA, the Trade Library and the British Chamber of Commerce. The new premises are packed with cd-roms, modems, information on British education services – even a special telephone to book flights to Britain. These arrangements have allowed the individual agencies to cut costs and increased their impact.

There are many extremely able and energetic people involved in these efforts. But the problem is that without a coherent, overall strategy, the whole may often be less than the sum of its parts. There is at present no central coordination, no common evaluation and no clear direction to ensure that the messages sent by Britain's political leaders, businesses and public agencies are in harmony.

Part 2. What is identity for?

Before addressing how we might think in a new way about our identity, it is worth asking why we need one. Britain is unlikely to be caught up in any major wars involving mass conscription. It no longer needs an identity strong enough to inspire young men to sacrifice their lives. Britain is doing well as a tourist destination and as a site for inward investment. Our firms, cities and even subcultures have strong identities in their own right and, in any case, it is far from obvious that a national identity is a useful thing. Most, after all, are grotesque caricatures anyway, Germany – ruthless efficiency, France – style, Spain – passion, and so on.

Traditionally, the case for a new identity has been made on political grounds. Some have argued that as communities break down (with even families becoming atomised), a new identity can act as a valuable social glue for holding polities together. Some see a strong sense of national identity as essential for legitimating the state and its capacity to take difficult decisions. Others have argued that national self-hatred is problematic, as nations at ease with themselves tend to have happier people and higher productivity, and find it easier to accept others.

These arguments are all powerful and well rehearsed, but there is a compelling new argument for taking identity seriously: the economic argument. If the different agencies of government and business work in tandem in projecting a positive identity, there are measurable benefits for the national economy. In what follows I set out the steps of this argument and show why national identities are valuable, how they are manageable, and what other benefits they can contribute.

The identity premium

The core argument for taking a strategic approach to national identity is that it creates an economic premium. Most of us know that
we are willing to pay more for products from some countries than
from others: we will pay over the odds for consumer electronics
from Japan, food products from Italy, engineering from Germany. A
Wolff Olins survey of 200 Fortune 500 companies showed that 72
per cent see national image as important in influencing their purchasing decisions. Many companies find it valuable to feed off
national image. Thus AEG has used the fact that it is a German company as the centrepiece of recent advertising campaigns – redefin-
ing the initials as 'Advanced Engineering from Germany'.

This link between nationality and marketability is not new. It was
what gave the label 'Made in Britain' economic value in the past. But
there is an argument that today national identity is becoming more
important.

The argument parallels that which is often made about corporate
identities. In the 1980s, as technological advancement meant that
the products of many different firms were no longer easily distin-
guishable in terms of objective qualities, companies tried to differentiate themselves by tapping into deeper emotions and cultivating
an identity which would make consumers more loyal and willing to
pay a premium for products. Those which were successful saw this
success translated into higher sales and higher profits. As a result,
the cultivation of identity is now a normal part of business practice.

Just as the differences between companies may be less than in the
past, so are the differences between countries. Most of the OECD
countries have a broadly similar capacity to produce quality products in a range of different fields. We no longer expect a product
from Spain or Korea to fall apart. As a result, just as good design can
provide a competitive edge, so can the broader associations of a
national identity differentiate products and services.

In opposition to this argument, it is often claimed that in an
increasingly global economy, country of origin is no longer an issue.
When the top 100 global companies have 40 per cent of their assets
abroad and when most products are made up of components from

several countries, the very idea of nationality may be obsolete. David Mercer, Head of Design at BT, put it this way: 'BT want to see themselves as a global company rather than as a national company. We want to see ourselves truly as an international company, which means operating as a German company in Germany, rather than as a British company in Germany, and as a Swiss company in Switzerland.'[59]

But in fact, BT's strategy has as much to do with the problems of Britain's identity as with the limits of national identity *per se*. Mercer admits that 'nearly ten years ago, British Telecom did research into the appropriateness of the name British Telecom in overseas markets. We found that we had problems with the name in certain parts of the world – Japan was a particular problem – where the name "British" was understood to stand for "of the past", "colonial", not about innovation, not about high technology, or the future or moving forward. Given the fact that we are in a fast-moving, highly innovative, creative area in telecommunications, the name British was a problem, and that was why we changed from British Telecom to BT. So national identity does influence the way that large companies do business overseas'.[60]

In other words, even in a genuinely global economy, national identity can provide a premium. Just as location in a prime 'industrial district' (such as Silicon Valley for information technology, the City of London for finance, Hollywood for film) confers all sorts of economic externalities, so does national origin provide intangible externalities to businesses.

These externalities can be understood as a premium: the difference in value of a product originating in a country which has successfully managed its identity compared to one from a country without a distinctive or attractive identity. In practice it is never easy to define this precisely: company brands interact with national identities in complex ways. But it is possible to map these 'identity premiums' and even to measure them in fairly systematic ways.

Figure 7 shows how it might be done for an imaginary country. Any nation has an identity in a number of dimensions. Germany for example is very strong on quality and innovation but weaker on creativity and service. Britain, as we have seen, has relatively strong ser-

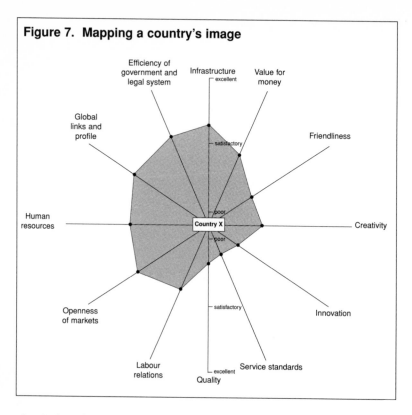

Figure 7. Mapping a country's image

vice industries but is not generally seen as innovative or excellent quality. As a result, German companies operating in sectors where quality and innovation are key will, *other things being equal,* have an advantage over British ones.

The value of these maps, which can be constructed out of systematic surveys of opinion in other countries, is that they provide a spotlight on strengths and weaknesses and a means of tracking progress in dealing with them. All countries must decide which parts of the identity map they would benefit most from occupying – whether to specialise heavily and simply play to their strengths or whether to attempt to develop a more rounded reputation.

Part 3. What are the tools for constructing an identity?

How have other countries managed their identities?

The need to shed outdated or unhelpful images is not a uniquely British preoccupation. In the past, many countries have tried to change their identity to mark a change of régime or a change of orientation. The motivations for these efforts differ greatly – from trying to bury uncomfortable historical memories (Germany after the war, Chile overcoming its 'junta' image, Spain post-Franco) to projecting modernity (Ireland shedding its rural Catholic image, New Zealand attempting to reduce its economic dependence on sheep), to re-establishing a link with the past (as with much of the former Soviet Union).

Many of these attempts have been strikingly successful, ranging from Japan's extremely concerted strategy to drop its image as a maker of cheap and shoddy products to Finland's much more recent rise as a powerhouse of IT. In this section I briefly describe some of the more interesting recent attempts to change national images and define a different 'national brand'.

> 'The British Council ... tends to steer away from the United States, preferring to go down old colonial routes ... We should go to Washington and take over the the National Gallery there. It is time to think big!'
>
> Phillip Dodd, Institute for Contemporary Arts

For Europeans, Spain offers one of the best examples of a concerted attempt to rebrand a country. There were many convergent aims: to shed the shadow of Franco; to move upmarket as a tourist destination (and shed the 'Costa' image); to provide a place for Spain's constituent parts, such as Catalonia; and to redefine Spain as a modern industrial nation, a serious player in the European Union and a democracy. The 'España' picture by Miro, which became the national logo, symbolised a bright, optimistic passionate Spain which contrasted with the buttoned up dourness of the Franco years. As an image it dovetailed perfectly with the rebirth of Barcelona as a vibrant European city and Spain's new political circumstances under a young and relaxed prime minister. Many different institutions – from the monarchy under Juan Carlos, to emerging multinationals like REPSOL – moved in the same direction to achieve a fundamental shift in perceptions, remaking Spain as a young country.[61]

Ireland offers a similar example. Like Spain, Ireland suffered from being seen as rural, Catholic and reactionary. Over twenty years its image has been transformed. Today it is seen as an exciting, innovative 'Celtic tiger', with Dublin recast as one of Europe's liveliest cities. Its success can be attributed to many factors, from a good education system and generous lures to inward investors to EU grants, but it has been helped by the clever use of culture – in particular attracting filmmakers (one of the strongest shapers of national identities today) – as well as smart marketing. Ireland's recently relaunched corporate identity is a symbol of two people greeting, symbolising both the rapprochement of North and South, and Ireland's identity as a friendly, welcoming country.

In Australia, the government undertook an equally ambitious programme to change its identity, using export promotion, inward investment campaigns and a series of projects around the Creative Nation project to rethink the place of Australia's aborigines and its relationship to its Asian neighbours. In the words of Greg Dyke, now chief executive of Pearson Television, 'Australia was seen as an Oceanic economy linked to the UK, the Queen and the class system. It is now seen as an Asian-Pacific country with historic links to the UK. The government turned the Labour Party on its head and turned it into an 'Enterprise Party' – then it started on the country.' Work on image, to take Australia beyond koalas and kangaroos, has gone hand in hand with practical steps, like attracting more Asians to Australian universities and research projects, and embedding Japanese inward investment in ambitious science and technology sites.

Other examples include France which has used 'Grands Projets' to modernise its identity and which has an extremely centralised machinery for managing identity; Chile which cleverly built on campaigns to sell Chilean Wine with campaigns claiming 'Chile, it's not just a bunch of grapes'; and Italy which has worked to reinforce its image as a 'capital of style'. According to one British observer: 'The Italian showrooms are just as you would expect them to be: clean-looking, slick, colourful, stylish. There is lots of money spent on the look by promotional experts. It is consistent from New York to Africa. Just compare the image of Italy as a political entity (a bit of a joke!) to it as a commercial entity, where it is far from a joke.' In Germany, by contrast, there is little official coordination, but the clarity and consistency among the population and business community about what the German brand stands for means that this matters little.

To this list we might add some of the cities which are increasingly managing their own brands. Examples range from New York (the 'Big Apple') to Barcelona, Helsinki to Adelaide, Glasgow to Manchester: all have developed brand identities to help attract industry, new investment and international sporting and cultural events

While the means used differ greatly, in all of these examples there has been a clear fit between the visions of the political, business and cultural communities and a common determination to bring the external image into line with what the people living in the country or city take most pride in.

Can one brand a country? Lessons from business

These examples of national branding exercises have gone in parallel with an explosion of new techniques for branding businesses. Many people object to the idea of nations having a 'brand'. They claim that national identities are far too complex and many-voiced, and that, in any case, it would be wrong for anyone to manage them. Yet in practice all modern nations, and many modern cities, manage their identities in ways that are not dissimilar to the management of brands by companies. Governments operate networks of offices, advertise, promote and choose particular images and particular readings of history and, as we have seen, spend large sums of money trying to get it right. So although business is very different, it would be surprising if there weren't important parallels and lessons to be learned.

The single most important lesson from business is that identities have to be about more than just public relations. They cannot provide only a thin veneer on the outside surface of a company. The successful national rebranding exercises mentioned above worked only because the new identity fitted with a changing reality. Spain really was becoming more open, modern and liberal. Ireland really was booming in new industries, from U2 to IT. Australia truly was becoming a more heterogeneous and less British nation. For private firms, too, there is no point trying to change an identity if the reality is left unchanged. If there is too large a gap between the identity and how, for example, staff behave to customers, or managers behave to staff, the result is hostility and cynicism. The dissonances become as visible as the identity itself.

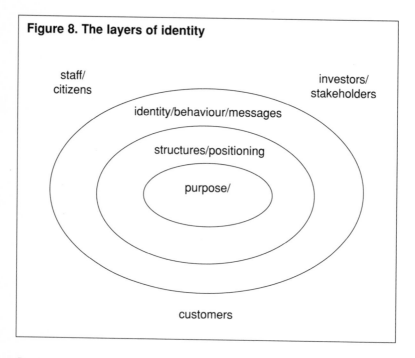

Figure 8. The layers of identity

staff/citizens

investors/stakeholders

identity/behaviour/messages

structures/positioning

purpose/

customers

Demos

This is why attention has turned to how identities need to be made coherent and to why ethos is as important as identity in shaping everything from how things look to how people behave.

According to this view, at the core of a firm, or a nation, are the values, principles and most cherished beliefs which hold the whole together. These provide the glue for corporate or social cohesion as well as being the source of people's motivation to act in a wider interest.[62]

At a second level are the architectures and positioning – the institutions which express identity, including parliaments, businesses, charities, as well as the positioning in an external environment.

Finally, at a third level there are the messages that are sent out, the forms of the identity (such as logos and flags) and the behaviour of staff and citizens.

> 'Companies spend the right amount of money promoting themselves and do it extremely well. This contrasts with the CBI and DTI which are homespun'
>
> Charles Trevail, Sampson Tyrrell

To transform a culture it is essential to begin by reaching agreement around the elements of a new ethos. In everything the organisation does, everything it owns and everything it produces, there should be a clear idea of what the organisation is and what its aims are. Only then can change take place in the two outer levels, with care to ensure that the structures and messages are consistent with the ethos. When they clash the identity falls into crisis: if, for example, a nation prides itself on honesty and its institutions are corrupt or if it prides itself on quality and its products are shoddy.

Within a company the best way to begin a process of transforming cultures, identities and ethos is to find out what people truly care about; what motivates them to contribute to the organisation; what they feel most proud about; which stories of the company's role animate them. Only when that ethos takes shape is it possible to think about the other elements of an identity, such as logos, flags and anthems. These come last, not first.

Usually companies' externally focused identity programmes of corporate branding – used to establish the corporate product, service or retail brand through names, visual symbols, packaging envi-

Figure 9. Twelve principles for culture changers

Be distinctive

Seventeen out of twenty new brands fail – usually because the brand doesn't offer the consumer anything new.[63] In a world where countries have very little 'brand recognition', it is vital to isolate a unique selling proposition.

Branding starts at home

If your identity is going to convince anyone outside the country, it has to be believed by people living in it.

Hype is unsustainable

No image which is fundamentally at variance with reality can be convincing.

Be simple

Although there can be a complex emotional or intellectual subtext, the basic brand proposition needs to be simple and credible.

Be strategic and repeat yourself

It takes time to change perceptions. After eighteen years of Thatcherism, people still see the economy as closed and strike-ridden. Research by the DTI shows that one-off initiatives have very little impact on attitudes. The basic message needs to be continually reinforced using different media in different contexts.

Soft touch

Hard sells are treated with extreme scepticism by sophisticated audiences.

Balancing continuity with change

You can't create something from nothing – all identities are based on history – even if they use it selectively. When Eastern European countries invented identities they all used things that were at least 200 years old.

Isolate givens from things to fight for

Some perceptions are already so entrenched and powerful that they do not need to be pursued, others are more up for grabs.

Diversity, but within coherent environment

The British story is obviously complex and must be inclusive enough for all agencies and people who live in Britain to buy into.

Go with the grain but also tackle negatives

It is wise to go with the grain of existing attitudes, but also to tackle head on any negative perceptions.

Set objectives and track progress

Identities should be managed with the same professionalism as other assets. None of the agencies currently charged with managing Britain's identity track it systematically.

Benchmark and know your enemy

Other countries are making rapid strides in improving and managing their identities. We should systematically keep an eye on best practices elsewhere.

ronments and so on – are matched by internal 'vision programmes'. Their purpose is to create in the minds of all stakeholders a clear idea of what the organisation is and what it stands for. Many such change programmes work only on the superficial elements. But as one practitioner put it 'identity is a contact sport', and unless the brand is experienced in a special way, no amount of smart imagery will substitute. So how British managers, police, hotel staff or airline personnel behave and view themselves is crucial to shaping the broader national identity. These are not easy to influence (although the Singapore government has tried to legislate for politeness and friendliness).

It is important to recognise that identities do not have to be monolithic. Some companies use a very tight consistent branding across all their activities. Virgin is a good contemporary example that now stretches from air travel to insurance. Others, like Nestlé, link different products through a graphical or written endorsement. Alternatively, companies like Unilever use a range of apparently unrelated brands. National identities probably best fit in the middle of this range. They should not be so consistent as to block out diversity. But nor are they just invisible containers of wholly separate corporate or regional identities.

Part 4. Shaping our identity

Stories that link the past and the future

Identities consist of more than images, flags, logos and ceremonials. Successful national identities are also shaped around compelling stories that make sense of where a nation has come from, and where it is going. In the past, Britain had no shortage of stories of this kind: the story of the chosen people, the island race, the defenders of freedom. In Part 2, I set out the six interwoven stories that have shaped the heritage of Britishness: the idea of Britain as a land of great and stable institutions, the imperial nation, the industrial powerhouse, home of the English language, the Protestant nation, and inventor of sport and fair play. Each of these stories differentiated us from other countries, had a historical pedigree and made a statement about Britain in the future. Together, they combined to support a meta-story of Britain as a unique imperial power, quite unlike other empires.

> 'The particular British challenge is learning to change without having a revolution, or being defeated in a war'
> Linda Colley

Today, as we have seen, these stories have lost their resonance. We need new stories that both reach back into our history and project forward into the future. In this chapter I set out some of the possible stories and ingredients which might form a new identity and the reality on which they can draw.

Hub UK – Britain as the world's crossroads
'Britain is an island, but it is never insular. It is more connected to the world than any land-bound nation. It is a hub: a place where

goods, messages and ideas are exchanged; a bridge between Europe and America, north and south, east and west.

This aspect of Britain helped to define the empire as much as a splash of pink on the map. Britain's empire was also a web of connections, from the transoceanic cables and radio links to the trading routes, and the financial exchanges of the City of London. Britain developed technology to link the world and speed it up: from the Cutty Sark and clipper ships to transoceanic calls, from the London underground to radio, from the early land and sea speed records to the steam engine and the jet engine, from the Stockton and Darlington Railway to Concorde.

This openness runs deep in our culture and imagery. Britain has always been open to immigration, more at ease with inward investment by German or Korean companies and open to cultural influences ranging from Indian food to Japanese manufacturing. The rich imagery of the sea has always been central to national identity – from the white cliffs of Dover to the great ports of Liverpool and Glasgow, from 'Heart of Oak' to Paul McCartney's folksy 'The Mull of Kintyre' or the imperial 'Rule Britannia'.

Today, Britain is more than ever a hub: the old links still exist and have been re-energised through membership of the European Union, the strength of industries like finance and telecommunications, our favourable position in the world's time zones and the success of the English language.

That place prepares Britain well for a new century. We are strong not just in the creative industries but also in the knowledge market – creating ideas, researching and importing and exporting students and materials. We are strong in the industries of speed and connections – with the world's third largest aerospace industry and dominance in Formula One racing and in telecommunications. Far from being unchanging or closed off, Britain is a country at ease with change, a place of coming and going, of import and export, of quickness and lightness.'

■ Heathrow is the world's busiest airport for international passengers. In 1994, Britain's civil airports handled a total of 123.9 million passengers.[64]

- British Airways is the largest airline in the world for international scheduled services, while Britannia Airways is the world's largest charter airline.
- Britain is leading the world in telecommunications. BT's turnover from international phone calls for the year ending 31 March 1996 was £1,000,980,000.
- In 1996, 14 million overseas tourists came to London, more than any other city in Europe.[65]
- After the United States, Britain is the most popular country in the world as a destination for secondary and tertiary education, attracting 285,000 international students in 1996, 20 per cent up on the previous year, as well as 740,000 language students. There are 10,000 doctors and health professionals from overseas training in Britain at any one time. British education and training exports are worth £7 billion a year.[66]
- The Edinburgh Festival is the largest international arts festival in the world – attended by 418,000 people in 1996. The Glastonbury Festival was attended by 90,000 people in 1997 and 240,000 people went to the Proms in 1996.
- Britain is the fifth largest trading nation in the world. Britain exports more per head than the United States and Japan.[67]
- The turnover of the London currency markets is greater than that of New York and Tokyo combined.[68]
- The City of London has 300 international banks and a workforce of 800,000, more than the entire population of Frankfurt.
- In 1994, 13,000 overseas companies were operating in Britain including more than 4,000 from the US, over 1,000 from Germany and 200 from Japan. Rover, Ford, Vauxhall, Peugeot-Talbot, Honda, Nissan and Toyota all choose to manufacture their cars in Britain. Overseas companies are responsible for 18 per cent of British manufacturing employment and 40 per cent of British exports.[69]
- Britain is first in Europe and second in the world only to the US as a destination for international direct investment, attracting US$325 billion in FDI in 1995. In 1995, Britain attracted 38.0 per

'If we've invented anything, it is speed! The steam engine, concorde, Formula One cars – we are a mobile nation'

Phillip Dodd, Institute for Contemporary Arts

cent of US investment and 40.4 per cent of Japanese investment into the EU, and even attracted the greatest share (15 per cent) of German investment in the world.[70]

■ Britain is second only to the United States as a source of outward investment, investing nearly $400 billion in 1995.[71] Overseas direct investment by British companies is nearly 3 per cent of UK GDP (compared with less than 1 per cent in Italy, France, Japan, Germany and the United States).[72]

■ Britain has produced some of the world's greatest explorers, such as Sir Walter Raleigh, Captain Cook, Scott of the Antarctic, Dr Livingstone, Sir Edmund Hillary and Ranulph Fiennes.

■ The BBC was one of the first broadcasting institutions with worldwide reach, broadcasting in English and 40 other languages around the world. It has a global audience of 133 million regular listeners and sells recorded programmes for radio to other broadcasters in over 100 countries. In 1994–95 BBC Worldwide Television licensed more than 14,500 hours of programming to over 80 countries around the world, making the BBC Europe's largest exporter of television programmes.

■ English has become the world's global language. It is spoken by around one in five of the world's population,[73] with over 1.4 billion people living in countries where English has official status.[74] In fact there has never been a language so widely spread or spoken as an official language by so many people. It is now widely used internationally as the main language for purposes such as air traffic control, academic and business gatherings, science technology, diplomacy, sport, international competitions, pop music, advertising, popular culture and the Internet. English is also the language of Microsoft and IBM.

■ A British company, Reuters, boasts the world's largest privately leased communications network to transmit its services. Reuters also wholly owns Reuters Television (RTV), the largest international television news agency in the world. RTV supplies news videos to over 200 broadcasters and their networks in 84 countries.

Creative island

'Britain is a peculiarly creative nation. We have a history of eccentricity and quirkiness, and an ethos that values individuality, nonconformity, new ideas and difference. This has been expressed in our culture, from Shakespeare to Turner, Dickens to Francis Bacon, Mary Wollstonecraft to Tom Paine. It is also manifest in the contemporary blossoming in film, design, architecture, music, computer games and fashion.

Creativity is a state of mind that is restlessly looking for new ways of doing things – whether that means a new genre for television, a new design for a vacuum cleaner or a shop, or a new insight into physics.

Cultivating that creativity requires us to remain a diverse, challenging society; resisting pressures to conformity; valuing the new even it if is disturbing; and seeing creative fields not as marginal but as central to our economic future. This is the story of Britain at the forefront of creativity and invention, leading the world across a range of disciplines – the story of a small island with big ideas.'

■ Britain has won 90 Nobel Prizes for science, second in number only to the United States and has a long tradition as a leader in scientific and technological discoveries – from Isaac Newton's gravitation and three laws of motion in the seventeenth century, through Charles Darwin's theory of evolution and Michael Faraday's electric motor, generator and transformer in the nineteenth century, to Stephen Hawking's work on the origin of the universe; Brian Josephson's on superconductivity; Martin Ryle and Anthony Hewish's on radio astrophysics and the discovery of the hole in the ozone layer by British Antarctic Survey scientists in the twentieth century.

'Once again Britain can claim to be leading the way. We can say with pride that we are the "design workshop of the world" – leading a creative revolution.'
Tony Blair, *The Guardian*

■ Britons pioneered medical advances, including the development of immunisation by Edward Jenner in the eighteenth century, the discovery of penicillin by Sir Alexander Fleming and the founding of antiseptic surgery by Lord Lister in the nineteenth century, the discovery of DNA by Watson and Crick, and Dorothy Hodgkin's discovery of cholesterol and insulin in the mid twentieth century and Alec Jeffreys' DNA fingerprinting, the identification of genes linked to diseases such as cystic fibrosis, the cloning of Dolly the sheep and Blatchford's development of articificial limbs in the 1990s.

'Creativity is not replicable – look at the tiger economies – so much economic muscle but no design base. Taiwanese cars are designed by RCA graduates'

Anneke Elwes, BMP DDB Needham

- According to MITI, 70 per cent of significant inventions and one fifth of all post-war inventions were made in Britain – British technological innovations have shaped the modern world from the first practical demonstration of television by John Logie Baird in 1926, through the invention of radio and the computer, to the fibreoptic cable.

- Britain is leading the world in the creation of computer games: 70 per cent of world's computer games are made within thirty miles of Liverpool. British software houses such as Cambridge Animation, Parallax systems, Virtuality and Superscape are world leaders.

- Design and related activity in Britain is worth £12 billion a year, employing more than 300,000 people; many of the world's largest international design consultancies are British and Britain ranks among the world's top five nations for design skills, according to a survey of design managers in large Japanese companies.[75]

- Nearly one third of the 30,000 student designers who graduate each year from Europe's design colleges are trained in Britain.[76]

- In fashion, Britons, all educated at London-based Central Saint Martin's College, run the fashion world's most illustrious houses: Stella MacCartney at Chloe, John Galliano at Christian Dior and Alexander MacQueen at Givenchy and London Fashion Week is now as important as its Paris and Milan equivalents, with leading designers such as Vivienne Westwood and models such as Naomi Campbell.

- Outstanding buildings at home and abroad, designed by British architects from Sir Norman Foster and Sir Richard Rogers to Piers

Gough, include Waterloo Station, the Berlin Reichstag and numerous football stadiums.

■ Britain is the world's centre for creative advertising with £10 billion spent on advertising a year.[77]

■ In 1994, nearly 17 million people in Britain attended events in one or more of the major art forms and Britain boasts some of the world's finest artists and sculptors, from Damien Hirst to David Hockney.

■ There has been a renaissance of the British film industry, with the success of such films as *Four weddings and a funeral* (the most successful British film ever, grossing more than £160 million world-wide), *Trainspotting* and *The English patient.*

■ Britain leads the world in animation, winning four Oscars in recent years with films like Nick Park's *The wrong trousers,* and a high proportion of world films have their technical creation, special effects and animation carried out by Britons.

■ Britain is one of the world's major centres for theatre, boasting the Royal National Theatre, the Royal Shakespeare Company, the English Stage Company at the Royal Court Theatre and training schools such as RADA, as well as a host of internationally recognised contemporary playwrights from Harold Pinter to David Hare.

■ The British music industry had a £1.1 billion turnover in 1996, making it the strongest export sector.

■ The British buy more music per head than any other nationality except for the Americans.[78]

■ British artists have long been leading the world in music and musical innovation – from the Beatles and Pink Floyd in the 1960s and 1970s to Oasis, Radio Head, Prodigy, Orbital, Portishead and the Spice Girls in the 1990s. The ethnic mix of West Indians and Asians has developed new types of music from dance music to trip-hop.

■ British musicals have a phenomenal success on Broadway and across the world. *Cats* has played in twenty different countries

'When we handed over Hong Kong ... There should have been a rock concert to celebrate Britain's departure, because that was probably our biggest contribution to Hong Kong, apart from our bankers, buildings and opium. That whole creative aspect ... is something we deal with very badly in Britain'

Peter Jenner,
Sincere Management

grossing £100,405,394 in the UK alone. *Jesus Christ superstar* has played in 37 different countries and *Les misérables* has played in 26.[79]

- Britain boasts the leading training centres for classical music: the Royal Academy of Music and the Royal College of Music, and modern British classical composers including Sir Michael Tippett and Sir Peter Maxwell Davies are some of the most innovative in the world.

- Each year, 650 professional arts festivals take place in Britain. The Edinburgh Festival and the Proms are the largest of their kind in the world.

- Last year, 80 million people visited galleries and museums in Britain.

- There were 100,000 new books published in 1996 and Britain has the largest export publishing industry in the world, worth over £1 billion a year.[80]

- The quality of the BBC is recognised the world over: it won two Oscars in 1996, five International EMIs in 1996, four Prix Italia Awards 1997, four awards at the Montreux Golden Rose Festival 1997, one at the Cannes Film Festival 1997, three at the Monte Carlo TV Festival Awards, fifteen at the International Wildlife Festival in Montana, four at the San Francisco International Film Festival and two at the Chicago Film Festival.

- British television productions raised £185 million in export earnings and continue to win many international awards.

- British comedy is particularly successful, producing comedians such as Tony Hancock, Peter Sellers, Benny Hill, John Cleese and Rowan Atkinson, whose Mr Bean is the biggest TV comedy export since Benny Hill. Mr Bean has been sold to 94 countries, from Australia and Bahrain to Venezuela and Zimbabwe.

- Once reputed for its very poor cuisine, London is now the world's culinary capital, with such leading restaurants as the River Café and Bibendum.

United colours of Britain

'Britain is a hybrid nation – always mixing diverse elements together into something new. Not a melting pot that moulds disparate ethnicities into a conformist whole, but a country that thrives on diversity and uses it to constantly renew and re-energise itself. Britain's royal family mixed together German, Danish and, more recently, Greek ancestry. Our most famous retailer (Marks and Spencer) was founded by Russian Jews. Some of our most successful authors, like Salman Rushdie, are drawn from former colonies. Our contemporary cuisine is a fearless hybrid of elements from other nations. Our popular music began by combining American rhythm and blues with the traditions of the English music hall. But it is not just ethnicities that are mixed – Britain is also the world's capital of ways of living, the home of happily co-existing subcultures – from punks and ravers to freemasons and gentlemen's clubs. Britain is the least pure of European countries, more mongrel and better prepared for a world that is continually generating new hybrid forms.'

> 'Even the English aren't the original inhabitants of England'
> Lord Conrad Russell

- Britain's ethnic composition is remarkably diverse: over 3 million people (5.5 per cent) describe themselves as belonging to a 'non-white' group. Among these, 891,000 (1.6 per cent) are black, 840,000 (1.5 per cent) are Indian, 477,000 are Pakistani (0.9 per cent), 163,000 are Bangladeshi (0.3 per cent), 157,000 are Chinese (0.3 per cent) and 488,00 (0.9 per cent) belong to other ethnic groups.
- Most of the world's religions are represented in Britain: 1.2 to 2 million Muslims, 320,00 Hindus, 300,000 Jews (the second largest number in Europe) and 300,00 Sikhs. There are also smaller communities of Baha'is, well over 400 Buddhist groups and centres, 30,000 Jains and Zoroastrians.
- The English language is a hybrid. Although it derives primarily from one of the dialects of Anglo-Saxon, it has been very greatly influenced by other languages, particularly, following the Norman conquest, by French.

Demos

- There is great regional and local diversity within Britain, with cuisine as varied as Cornish pasties and Scottish haggis. Even London is a network of villages.
- Britain's wide ethnic diversity is also reflected in the extraordinary range of food we eat. Indian cuisine is an integral part of our culinary, turning over more than coal, steel and shipbuilding combined, and employing over 70,000 people.
- Chicken Tikka is one of Marks and Spencer's biggest exports.
- Many diverse subcultures thrive here: from punks and mods and rockers to ravers, and from working men's clubs to modern music clubs.
- In 1997, 200,000 people attended Gay Pride, making it one of the largest such events in the world.

Open for business

‘Britain has always been ‘a nation of shopkeepers’ and is today more than ever. British companies not only dominate the market with the rapid globalisation of many supermarkets, they are also constantly innovating and reinventing what retailing means. Shops like Habitat, Jigsaw on Bond Street and Prêt-à-Manger have reinvented the design of public space, and companies like the Body Shop have led the world in ethical trading. Britain has a highly developed service economy and one which is moving ahead in terms of providing services 24 hours, online as well as face to face. As services go global, whether in the form of insurance or call centres, Britain is better placed than any other European country to benefit and has the opportunity to turn customer service into a competitive asset. Margaret Thatcher led a crusade to encourage a society in which people would be ready to take risks and start their own businesses. Today a large proportion of young people would like to become self-employed, and businesses and services no longer have the stigma that the aristocracy (and more recently the public sector professionals) sought to attach to them. We have become a country of entrepreneurs, open to the rest of the world and constantly inventing new ways of doing business.’

- Services now account for approximately two thirds of the UK GDP compared with one half in 1950.[81]
- In 1996, retail sales accounted for almost a quarter of UK GDP. The economic contribution of retailers to those sales (as opposed to producers and wholesalers) accounted for some 10 per cent of GDP. The turnover of the retail sector in 1995 was £148,529 million.
- The retail sector employs 2.3 million people, a Full Time Equivalent of 1.7 million or 10 per cent of the workforce. Growth in retailing employment was the strongest of any sector as the UK came out of recession in the early 1980s and 1990s.
- Britain has more shop workers than France and Germany.[82]
- In 1993, there were 202,000 retail businesses in Britain, with 306,000 outlets.[83]
- There are already 286 Marks and Spencer stores around the UK, collectively taking more than £120 million a week. Tesco has put down roots in Poland and Hungary. Kingfisher, which owns Woolworth's, B&Q and Comet, has extended its continental operations from France to Belgium. Even Argos, the uniquely British catalogue company, is planning to open shops in the Netherlands.
- Eight out of ten most profitable European retailers are British.
- Two out of the top 25 global retailers are from the UK. Our only other European competitors represented are Germany, France and Holland.
- Four of the ten largest food retailers in Europe are British.[84]
- First Direct was the first telephone banking service in Europe.
- There has been a growth in ethical business in Britain with investors like the Co-op, Shared Interest, Trade Craft, Friends Provident and retailers like the Body Shop, which was set up in 1976 with a small store in Brighton selling 25 products. Today they have 1200 outlets in 45 countries. The company is valued at £365 million. Body Shop's success is clearly based on a combination of ethical trading (concern for human rights and the environment, opposition to animal testing) and aggressive international expansion – 80 per cent of its outlets are outside the UK.

Britain as silent revolutionary

'Far from being a nation of unchanging tradition, Britain is a prolific inventor of new forms of organisation and new ways of running society. It has contributed more social innovations to the world than any other nation – and is still doing so. From the municipal utilities to the health service, from modern charity to privatisation, and from the meritocratic civil service to the ethical multinational, Britain has been a silent revolutionary, quietly creating new ways of life – then reinventing them. Even the most traditional concerns – such as our attachment to the countryside and the idea of a 'green and pleasant land' – have been radically reinvented: new forms of organic farming have been pioneered by the Prince of Wales among others, ambitious reforestation schemes are being implemented throughout the country, new species are being reintroduced and Britain has some of the toughest measures to combat global warming. Britain is not a street-fighting nation, but its silent innovations have had as much impact as any revolutionary.'

- Britain was first in (and first out) of the industrial revolution.
- It was the first country to carry out democratic nationalisation and privatisation.
- Britain's political philosophy and ideas have had an influence the world over.
- British-style parliamentary democracy has been copied by countries throughout the world from India to South Africa.
- Our civil service model has been exported to countless countries. Over 100 countries sent delegations to the Cabinet Office in 1996–97 to study Britain's experience of public service reform.[85]
- Britain pioneered public infrastructure. Britain's welfare state has been emulated by countries the world over – from Mauritius to New Zealand.
- The Post Office, founded in 1635, pioneered postal services and was the first to issue adhesive postage stamps as proof of advance payment for mail.
- Britain has also led the way in the liberalisation of telecommunication and energy markets.

Demos

■ Britain boasts one of the most modern and well-trained professional armies in the world – even the French are modelling their armed forces on the British model.

■ Other institutional exports include the City and Insurance companies, law, universities (including the Open University), and of course the English language.

■ Britain has pioneered a huge number of modern sports. Modern tennis originated in 1872, with the first championships at Wimbledon in 1877. Rugby union football originated at Rugby School in the nineteenth century. Snooker was invented by the British in India in 1875. Table tennis, developed in the second half of the nineteenth century. Squash derives from rackets invented at Harrow School in the 1850s. Hockey was started by the Hockey Association (of England), founded in 1886. Golf originated in Scotland. The basic rules for cricket were drawn up in 1835 by the Marylebone Cricket Club. Badminton takes its name from the Duke of Beaufort's country home, Badminton House.

■ There are thousands of planning permission applications to convert train stations into art galleries and Victorian schools and warehouses into flats. Areas such as Docklands and Covent Garden have reinvented themselves – converting disused wastelands into to vibrant public spaces. This stands in stark contrast to Singapore where after twenty years of existence buildings have to be demolished.

■ The state is reforming itself, devolving power to the regions and the localities, and inventing new forms of supranational governance through its membership of the European Union.

■ Our parliamentary system is being reinvented with the most ambitious programme of constitutional reform this century.

■ Even Oxbridge is updating itself slowly, accepting a greater proportion of students from state schools and women.

'The cliché of Britain as an island of political and social stability in a world of change was always false ... Both the rhetoric of self-congratulation and self-flagellation have missed out how much Britain has changed since 1945. Britain has undergone three periods of revolutionary change. The Attlee government created the post-war society of entitlement, the 1960s created a new sexual, moral and aesthetic culture, and the Thatcher revolution sought to undo the first two and create a new society of achievement. Two revolutions and a counter-revolution'

Michael Ignatieff, *Prospect*

Demos

The nation of fair play

❝Britain is a team. Its self-image is based on a spirit of fair play, national solidarity, public service and support for the underdog. Unlike other countries which have relied on 'trickle down' or gloried in 'rough justice', Britain has been at the forefront of mechanisms to give people a 'fair go at life'. The institutions it has created – from the Beveridge welfare state to modern charity – have been central to the way it sees itself and conducts its business. It is a country of 'social entrepreneurs' with half its adult population taking part in voluntary sector activities. Its caring institutions enjoy universal support – with new ones being set up by all sections of the population from pop stars to politicians and Royals to business tycoons.❞

- We created the NHS and developed one of the most comprehensive welfare systems in the world.
- Up to half of all adults, in the course of a year, undertake some form of activity in the hundreds of thousands of voluntary organisations in Britain, ranging from international and national bodies to small local groups.
- Oxfam was founded in 1942 and had an income of £89.2 million in 1995–96 – it was one of the world's first major organisations dedicated to the relief of famine.[86]
- Live Aid, Band Aid, Feed the Children, and Children in Need have pioneered new forms of fundraising.
- Amnesty International was founded in 1961 and has a British membership of 138,548 (June 1997).[87]
- Friends of the Earth, founded in Britain in 1971, the second country to set it up after the US, now has a membership of 200,000 in Britain.[88] Greenpeace has a membership of 380,000,[89] The National Trust 2,293,000, The Royal Society for the Protection of Birds 890,000, and WWF for Nature has 219,000 members.[90]
- In 1996, twice as many Britons belonged to an environmental organisation or a charity as to a political party.[91]
- In 1996, Britain raised £2 billion in overseas aid, the sixth most generous in the world in terms of volume, (but only 0.26 per cent of GDP, placing Britain tenth in the world).

■ Individuals donate £6.1 billion to charity per annum, roughly £20 per head of the adult population. [92]

■ Charities have received £1.3 billion from the National Lottery.

The toolkit

Together, these six stories amount to a toolkit for a new sense of identity. They are like interlinking circles and complement each other to form a new story of Britain as a creative hub in an interconnected world, one that is founded on principles of tolerance and fair play. They should be our trademarks – at the heart of all promotional activity as we start the new century.

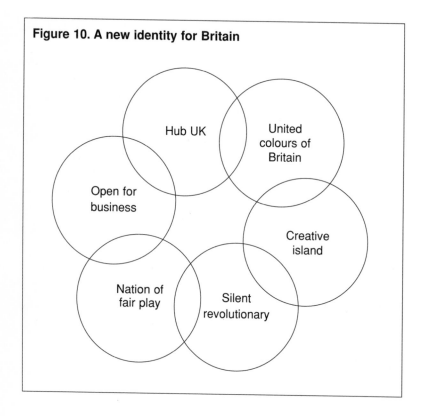

Figure 10. A new identity for Britain

Hub UK

United colours of Britain

Open for business

Creative island

Nation of fair play

Silent revolutionary

Part 5. Projecting a new identity

In preceding sections, I made the case for taking national identity seriously and highlighted some of the powerful economic benefits that stand to be gained. I argued that Britain needs a clearer, more forward-looking identity – not to reduce a diverse reality into a single image, but rather to provide a better vessel in which a wide range of industries can prosper in global markets. In this chapter I turn to how this could be done.

Encouraging a national consensus

The first priority is to cultivate a national consensus. Just as the new identity that was forged in the late eighteenth and early nineteenth centuries was born out of public debate and argument, today we need the widest possible participation in rethinking our identity. Some of that debate is happening already, sparked off by devolution and further moves to European integration, by the handover in Hong Kong and the growing confidence of many of Britain's ethnic minorities.

But there is still a long way to go and few have made the link between the political and cultural aspects of identity and their economic significance – the 'identity premium' that flows to businesses when the national identity is being managed well. Instead, the identity we will take with us into the new century remains ambiguous and the agencies charged with managing it are often confused about the messages they are conveying.

Achieving greater clarity will require a lead from the top. A small high level 'vision group' bringing together a few key players from business, the arts and diplomacy could be established under the chairmanship of the Prime Minister to agree strategic objectives for Britain's identity and to assess whether these objectives are being met. A vision group of this kind could set in motion a wider national debate about the messages and images that Britain should be projecting.

Reforming our institutions

If we are to treat our identity as an important asset, it needs to be managed professionally. Without new structures to define, refine and project what Britain is about, our efforts will continue to be at best fragmented and at worst contradictory.[93]

'National identity is not an intellectual or advertising problem – it is a machinery of government problem'

Adrian Ellis, AEA consultants

There is at present no central body with an overall responsibility for the management of our identity. As a result, there is no single message being relayed to the outside world, no coherent strategy, no systematic evaluation and a good deal of duplication both in research and implementation.

Working under the vision group, there will need to be a larger working party in which all the relevant agencies – DTI, British Council, FCO, Invest in Britain, trade associations, business and trade unions – are represented. This working party would be charged with ensuring that consistent messages are being used and with providing consistent monitoring of how Britain's image is evolving around the world, and how negative and positive perceptions are changing.

To provide a means of achieving strong central coordination and to link the work of the vision group and a larger body, a new unit could be established in the Cabinet Office, since it alone has the authority to coordinate the work of different departments and agencies. A small 'Promoting Britain Unit' could ensure:

■ a focused discussion on how Britain's strengths can be distilled into key themes and close liaison on their use

- a central capacity coordinating forward plans for promotional activity so that opportunities for cumulatively reinforcing messages are not squandered
- a central information source responsible for the dissemination of briefing material, best practice, case studies, thematic material and so on
- advice on effective commissioning of events and activities
- a determined attempt to coordinate cross-departmental activity so that exhibitions, speakers, events and roadshows can be used in more than one context
- a campaign to encourage other institutions to work in tandem with government agencies and departments
- a 'brand space' where people can go to absorb values, vocabulary, imagery and re-energise their conceptions of the national brand
- support for cities and regions in developing their own identities.

The challenge will be to set up a framework that will effectively coordinate what we do while also leaving organisations sufficient freedom to create and transmit messages to their target audiences – which may range from elderly German tourists to Chinese entrepreneurs.

Once a central body has been given a remit to manage our identity, it will be possible to professionalise our activities. Some of the methods used by global companies to manage their corporate identities can be usefully taken up to ensure clarity and consistency for the whole 'corporate' image of the UK, from embassies and British Council offices to promotional literature and news services. Strategies of this kind need to be implemented over a number of years and part of their value is to replace a 'one-off' culture with a more systematic approach to everything from advertising campaigns to trade shows. They also need to be based around clear criteria for performance measurement, for example establishing a baseline of current levels of awareness and perceptions within key countries and then revisiting them annually (so far, this has only been done in India).

The corollary of new approaches to external identity is a shift in the cultures of the agencies charged with presenting the UK to the outside world. Some of the necessary steps might include:

- changing recruitment policies so that the most entrepreneurial, not the brightest, are employed
- setting regular performance targets for staff
- deliberately employing members of Britain's ethnic minorities
- establishing an awareness training programme so that those responsible for selling Britain abroad understand the key messages, believe in them and have sufficient knowledge of Britain's strengths in design, technology and innovation to talk about them with conviction
- establishing a cadre of British design and creative ambassadors able and willing to travel the world and articulate Britain's strengths.

In all of this it is vital that we encourage creativity. Official forms of communication do not have to be pompous or dull. They can reflect the best of creative thinking and there is no reason why they cannot be playful, ironic, self-parodying and fun. Indeed, the more they can achieve a slightly irreverent tone the more they will project an image of modernity and dynamism. Unfortunately, far too much that emanates from Britain and its official institutions still reeks of arrogance and self-importance.

'Ambassadors used to be people with plumed hats, but now we need top-class salesmen – we've got to make the FCO realise that the cocktail days are over'
Lord Archer of Weston-super-mare

The targets for activity of this kind need to be carefully chosen. Many of the activities of the British Council and other organisations have been aimed at former colonies or middle-ranking countries which are not central to Britain's future in the world. We should have the confidence to target programmes of events, conferences, art exhibitions and performances at the key centres of influence – Washington, Tokyo, Berlin, Brussels – to inspire them with a new idea of Britain that can stretch all the way from the visual arts to product design.

Demos

The millennium as a focus

With measures of this kind under way, the millennium will provide an ideal early opportunity to project a new identity to the world and one that combines several anniversaries, including the two hundredth anniversary of the first use of the Union Jack and the one hundred and fiftieth anniversary of the Great Exhibition.

The greatest challenge of the millennium is not just to develop compelling experiences and objects to store under the dome or to amass a collection of hardware as in 1851 and 1951. If the millennium is to achieve its greatest impact, it will need to focus on values and ethos and how we are to get through the next century. It is worth remembering that the Great Exhibition of 1851 was not just an exhibition of Britishness – it was conceived by Prince Albert as a presentation of liberalism and *internationalism*. Those values remain relevant today and are in many ways much better suited to the twenty first century than the images of Britain that prevailed in the century after 1851.

For us, the millennium therefore represents a chance to reaffirm our sense of ourself as a global, open, tolerant island. In practical terms, that means a concerted effort to rethink our links with the rest of the world – whether they are personal, trading or communications links. These are a few of the steps that might be taken each of which express at least one of our stories for Britain in the next century:

> 'National identity is not just about what a country is successful at, or what makes it unique ... We should look instead at what we have in common with people outside Britain and what we can offer them. It's what you give to others which forges an identity'
>
> Theodore Zeldin

- We should make the points of entry and exit to Britain express the values of our renewed national identity. As a nation without lengthy land borders, we have the advantage that almost all visitors to Britain arrive and leave through a handful of locations. Too many of these are dominated by empty space and cold walls, and the shops that inhabit them are unimaginative and trinkety. The spectacular view of the white cliffs of Dover that greeted incoming ferries has been replaced by the featureless grey walls and fences that adorn the Eurostar's route, and our airports have no distinguishing features. Even architecturally impressive buildings like the Eurostar terminal in Waterloo or Stansted airport are cluttered with uninspiring retail outlets. We should house art exhibitions, museums and libraries in airports and stations to provide a stunning welcome for people arriving in the country and bring them into immediate contact with the best in contemporary art and design. We must develop efficient and easy to use transport links with clear ticketing and signs (in foreign languages as well as English) to transport visitors quickly to where they want to go. First impressions are also moulded by the first people you meet on entering a country (airline staff, immigration officials and so on) and they should be well trained, friendly, efficient and multilingual. Finally, the food industry and other private business could team up with the BAA to greet all arriving passengers with a mouthful of British food – from Scottish to Chinese, Balti to roast beef.

■ In the future, for an increasing number of countries, the main ports of entry will be electronic. Most governments have their own web sites, but they are usually rather dull collections of official information. Some cities have been much more innovative. Amsterdam has led the way with its digital city that provides not just useful information, but also 'cafés' for chat, culture, and billboards, all structured around the city's squares. An imaginative early step would be to create a digital Britain site, with links to individual cities (many of which already have their own sites) and including not just official information but listings, specially commissioned web art and discussion sites.

■ Government buildings in the UK and across the world should act as a showcase for Britain as a creative island. Some excellent new buildings have been commissioned in recent years. But many feel like hangovers from the empire, aspiring to look like eighteenth century stately homes. Government should also use our unique creative talents to redesign stamps, letterheads, public buildings, official documents and even our parliament, so that they too show off the best of British design.

- Government should highlight the best successes of private, voluntary and public sectors to demonstrate Britain's strengths to the world. Just as the Design Council's 'Millennium Products' initiative will highlight the best new products and services created in Britain, challenges should be issued to find other national successes as we approach the millennium, for example the best educational practices and institutions, the most innovative social entrepreneurs, the best city improvements.

- To consolidate Britain's position as a 'clever island' – a leading player in the global market for ideas – our universities should be given support to establish joint ventures and research institutes across the developing world (just as Australian universities have done in South East Asia).

- To broadcast the new Britain to the world, we should, even if only temporarily, increase even further support for film-making in the UK. Film is the most powerful medium for transforming national identities as the US has long understood and as more recently countries as diverse as Ireland and Spain have appreciated.

- To highlight our strengths as a 'nation of fair play', we should establish an online 'Commitments' site in the millennial dome, giving people immediate access to volunteering and mentoring organisations – so they can commit to spending time volunteering or mentoring in the new millennium, whether in the UK or abroad.

- We should not only highlight Britain's place in the world, but the world's place in Britain, by organising exhibitions of art and design by all the ethnic communities, commissioning the best impresarios from places like Trinidad and Rio to organise events across the country, and involving all of Britain's ethnic groups in public festivals to celebrate Britain's hybridity. Indeed, the millennium would be a good opportunity for Britain to listen to the rest of the world rather than proclaiming our own achievements too loudly.

- For a country with as distinctive a military history as Britain it is not surprising that our relations with other countries are not as good as they could be. Many will respect British democracy and the rule of law, but resent our arrogance and insensitivity. A truly bold step to rekindle our relationships, particularly with the great burgeoning nations of Asia, would be for the reigning monarch to use the millennium to visit all the major sites in the world where there is still bitterness over Britain's past, healing memories of everything from the Opium Wars in China to the legacies of the empire, from Africa and the Caribbean to Iran and Ireland. Both Germany and Japan have been forced into actions of this kind, but precisely because decolonisation was relatively untraumatic for Britain, there has been no thoroughgoing signal that Britain is no longer an imperial power. The millennium provides an ideal opportunity to rebuild a host of former imperial links as relationships based on reciprocity.

To these could be added many other practical steps that could be taken to crystallise a new identity in the world's eyes. To work, they will need to be shaped and owned by many different groups, not just national government but also perhaps a new generation of city mayors; not just business but also the arts; not just the makers of physical things but also the shapers of the new virtual realities of cyberspace.

Renewing Britain's identity will be a slow burn, not a quick fix. But, if we start now, it will not be long before some of the benefits start to flow and within a generation we could again be seen as one of the world's pioneers rather than as one of its museums.

Demos

Conclusion: re-imagining Britain

The multiple inventions of the eighteenth and nineteenth centuries are a useful reminder that national identities are neither unchanging or natural. They are invented – and reinvented – over periods of time, in response to changing demands and opportunities. Today, if we are living in the shadow of an older identity, it is not because this identity is somehow more authentic than any other. It is rather because the original invention of Britishness was so successful – providing a framework for Britain's rise to empire and industrial predominance – that it has proven extraordinarily difficult to update it.

Only one recent leader has been interested in thinking about national identity. Margaret Thatcher saw herself as a descendant of Boadicea and Queen Elizabeth I. She wanted the nation to take pride once again in its trading strength, its enterprise. And she sought, in the traditional way, to define the nation through identifying its enemies – from the liberal establishment of institutions with 'British' in their name to working-class miners, from immigrants to General Galtieri. For a time her sheer charisma seemed to be recasting the nation in her image. Britain's stock around the world certainly rose. Yet in retrospect we can see that she largely failed. Her image of Britain was too nostalgic, too bound up with empire, too exclusive and, little more than five years after posters proclaimed that the great had been put back into Britain, a survey showed that half the population wanted to emigrate.

Some will argue that identities are still as much about who you are against as what you are, and that it is impossible to have an identity that is open to the world. But today identities are worn more lightly than in the past – we may play at hating the French and

Germans, but we are happy to eat their food and buy their products; we are comfortable cooperating with their governments and doing business with them. In fact the world is ready for new forms of identity and will not tolerate the exclusive nationalism of the past.

Renewing Britain's identity does not mean inventing a completely new image of Britain or doing away with its heritage and tradition. It means regalvanising excitement around Britain's core values – as a democratic and free society in an interconnected world – and finding a better way of linking pride in the past with confidence in the future.

The time is ripe for action. There is a real sense that Britain is entering a new era. Its identity took shape during the long summer of the empire that lasted from 1851 to 1914. There then followed an autumn of slow decline until the 1960s and something more like a winter during the 1970s, 1980s and early 1990s with industrial conflict and the collapse of old industries. Throughout that period we clung on to our old identity as a reassuring certainty and a source of pride, at a time when Britain's power and influence were in retreat.

Now that period is over. Britain will never again be a superpower or an empire. But its position has stabilised as a major industrial and political power. It can never be a 'young country' in a literal sense, but it is bursting with the energy and excitement that young countries enjoy. Britain is now ready for its spring, a period of renewal and increased self-confidence.

Notes

1. British Tourist Authority, 1997, *Family of brands research report*, BTA, London.

2. See note 1.

3. See note 1.

4. Central Office of Information, 1996, *Britain 1996: an official handbook*, HMSO, London.

5. Anneke Elwes, 1994, *Nations for sale*, BMP DDB Needham, London.

6. See note 5.

7. See note 5.

8. See note 5.

9. British Council Statistics

10. See note 5.

11. See note 5.

12. See note 5.

13. Time International, 1993, *EURO-IMAGE studies*, Time International, New York/London.

14. See note 13.

15. See note 5.

16. See note 5.

17. Michael Porter, The Competitive Advantage of Nations, Macmillan, 1990

18. Henley Centre, cited in Elwes, 1994 (see note 5).

19. Wolff Olins, 1995, *Made in the UK*, Wolff Olins, London.

20. See note 19.

21. See note 19.

22. See note 19.

23. See note 19.

24. See note 19.

25. See note 19.

26. See note 19.

27. See note 13.

28. Synergy Brand Values Ltd, *Insight 96: a survey into social change*, BMRB, London.

29. See note 28.

30. See note 28.

31. It should be noted, however, that Britishness has never been an equal arrangement. Wales underwent a very different process of integration into the Union from Scotland, as the English language and law were imposed through an act of incorporation rather than established with consent through an act of Union. This is reflected in the fact that Wales is not even represented in the Union Flag.

32. For a full discussion of the construction of modern Britain, see Colley L, *Britons: forging of a nation*.

33. For a discussion of all these issues see Hobsbawm E, *Invention of tradition*.

34. Willets D, 1992, *Modern conversatism*, Penguin, London.

35. MORI, BPO survey, December 1995.

36. See note 35.

37. Henley Centre, 1996, *Planning for social change 1996-97*, Henley Centre, London.

38. MORI, 1994, *Public Opinion*

Newsletter, MORI, London.

39. See note 35.

40. Simon Winchester, interviewed on Australian Broadcasting Corporation's Late Night Live.

41. Joyce E, 1997, *Arms and the man: renewing the armed services*, Fabian Society, London

42. *New Statesman*, July 1997.

43. Jowell et al, eds, 1996, *British social attitudes: the 13th report*, Social and Community Planning Research and Darmouth Publishing, Aldershot.

44. Research by Bozell and Gallup cited in Smith D, 1997, 'Better made in Britain' in *Management Today*, January 1997.

45. See note 44.

46. See note 44.

47. See note 43.

48. See note 43.

49. NOP 1996

50. See note 43

51. See note 43.

52. For example, AC Milan, who were briefly forced to be 'Milano' during the Fascist era.

53. Hobsbawm E, 1990, *Nations and nationalism*, Cambridge University Press, Cambridge.)

54. See note 43.

55. See note 28.

56. See note 4.

57. AEA Ltd, *Excellence by design*, unpublished report, AEA Ltd, London.

58. Data taken from relevant organisations' annual reports and press releases.

59. Interview with David Mercer, July 1997.

60. See note 59.

61. There are some intriguing parallels with the UK, and not just because the Basques and the IRA actually carried out each other's killings in the 1970s. Spanish Historians have shown us the way: they have proved that, in 1640, Spain was just a vague geographical expression – it was no more of a state than Europe. In the seventeenth century there were still customs barriers between Castille and Aragon, different coronations, different currencies (same denomination, different values), separate councils and parliaments, separate legal systems, different constitutional systems, and the empire belonging to Castille and Aragon was not allowed to trade with it. Castille was a unitary state, whereas Aragon was decentralised. There was a massive row because Carlos V didn't find the time for his Valencian coronation till ten years later on. What began to bind Spain together was war – there was a Union of Arms in 1627. But several centuries of decline then followed with the loss of the colonies, invasion, royal feuds, civil war and dictatorship.

62. This section draws on some of the ideas of Norman Strauss among others (see *Missionary government*, *Demos Quarterly*, issue 7).

63. Blackett, T, 1997, 'Name that brand: developing new brands' in *British Brands*, issue 4, summer 1997

64. See note 3, 307

65. Llewelyn-Davies, UCL Barlett School of Planning and Comedia, 1996, *Four world cities: a comparative study of London, Paris, New York and Tokyo*, Department of the Environment and the Government Office for London, London.

66. Information from British Council press office.

67. See note 4.

68. In April 1995, London's Financial Exchange Markets had an average daily turnover of $464 billion, more

than the $244 billion for New York
and the $£161 billion for Tokyo com-
bined. See Llewelyn-Davies et al, 1996
(note 65).

69. See note 4, 212.

70. Invest in Britain Bureau, unpublished presentation.

71. OECD, 1995 cited in Invest in
Britain Bureau presentation.

72. *Financial Times*, 11 August 1995.

73. David, Graddol, 1997, *The future of
English*, The British Council, London.

74. Design Council, 1997, *The contribution of design to the economy*, Design
Council, London.

75. See note 74.

76. Netherlands Design Institute cited
in Central Office of Information, 1996
(see note 4).

77. See note 4.

78. Information from British
Phonographic Industry press office.

79. Information from Cameron
Macintosh and the Really Useful
Company press offices.

80. See note 4.

81. See note 4, 151.

82. Corfield I and Welch P, 1997, *Sold
short: government and retailing*, Fabian
Society, London.

83. See note 4, 227.

84. See note 4, 227.

85. See note 66.

86. Oxfam 1996 Annual Report,
Oxfam, Oxford.

87. Amnesty UK 1996 Annual Report,
Amnesty International, London.

88. Friends of the Earth UK 1996
Annual Report, Friends of the Earth,
London.

89, Office for National Statistics, 1997,
Social trends, HMSO, London.

90. See note 89.

91. See note 89.

92. Charities Aid Foundation, 1997,
Dimensions of the voluntary sector, CAF,
London.

93. Some of these ideas come out of
conversations and correspondence
with Wally Olins and are based on his
experience of working for the
Portugese government.